# PAYING IT
# BACKWARD

*— a memoir —*

# PAYING IT BACKWARD

How a Childhood of
Poverty and Abuse Fueled
a Life of Gratitude
and Philanthropy

## TONY MARCH

—— WITH ——

## MARVIN KARLINS

**Forefront**
BOOKS

Cover design, jacket, and book interior design
by Ray Kuik & Todd Krostewitz.

A special "Thank you!" to the never-ending patience
of the creative team at Q-Power Communications.
Their God-is-in-the-detail approach and unflinching support
ensured this endeavor would result in a treat for all readers.

# DEDICATION

*To Gail, my best friend and partner for most of my life. You reached into my darkness and taught me how to love. If my life has meant anything to anyone over the past four decades, it's only because you showed me how to open my heart.*

*To Mrs. Harris, Mrs. Aumiller, Mrs. West, and Mrs. Keyes—my HAWKs who took me under their wings and taught me to fly. You gave a poor, hungry, abused, and neglected boy the two tools he needed to not only survive but thrive: encouragement and education. I will never stop working to make you proud.*

*To Paul Laffin, my friend and mentor at Hartford's Mercy shelter. I will never forget what you taught me about serving and loving "the least of these." I think of you every time I give to charity or walk through the doors of a homeless shelter. Your life on earth was cut too short, but I pray your life of service lives on in me.*

# CONTENTS

# FOREWORD

There are some stories that can kick-start a morning, give perspective to a day, or provide hope in a challenging season of life. And there are other stories that can take us away to an imaginary place in our minds.

Every now and again, however, there is a story that takes our breath away and makes us think about what it's all about in the first place.

This is that story.

I first had the privilege of meeting Tony March in 2019, although I had heard a lot about him earlier from a good friend of mine and was curious to learn more.

Some of my interest was derived from the fact that, as the President of FranklinCovey Education, I am always excited to meet people whose lives were changed through education. And some of it simply was, I'm an unabashed fan of a great mission impossible story.

Growing up as a kid in the kind of poverty that would make most completely rethink the idea of being "poor," Tony found a way to dig deep within himself and outlast a dozen years of daily dumpster diving on the road to making a commitment to himself to never being poor again.

All this, while being faced with the daily challenges of a being a young black man in the 60s and 70s in an America that was not yet ready to consider equality a thing for every citizen.

What Tony credited as the ultimate catalyst in his rising

above poverty, abuse, racism, and a dysfunctional family life, on the road to becoming a leading engineer with General Motors (three U.S. patents to his credit) and the eventual owner of 21 car dealerships in seven U.S. states, didn't surprise me.

"Education," he shared simply.

In Tony's own words, "If it were not for the love, attention, and dedication of four key and influential teachers from grade school through high school," whom he refers to as The HAWKs, "my career path and life would have taken a dramatically different turn from that which I was blessed to have lived. It certainly wasn't a typical all-American white- or even blue-collar reality for me. I was so used to working harder, longer, and more intently than many of my fellow classmates and peers, that my loveless upbringing, in some sense, actually helped me, fueled me. I was so desperate to be loved, appreciated, and respected that all I was looking for was to be accepted."

What so many of us take for granted, Tony had to focus on as a daily mission, simply to survive.

I am often asked to speak on the power of education and its role in helping to provide opportunity for all. Tony's story will be one I enthusiastically reference often. Not only because he overcame impossible obstacles and odds on his road to extraordinary achievement, but more so, because as a fragile and vulnerable young boy, he believed that education could be his way out. His way out of the "black box," as he shares, and a life that was destined to repeat an old family cycle.

Tony March is a living example of channeling a burning

desire to leave an old world behind, while proactively forging a new paradigm and reality for himself, one that would see him becoming a leader on the world stage and making a difference in the lives of thousands.

Tony's story is ultimately not one of becoming extraordinarily wealthy and overcoming the odds, however. Rather, it's a much more intimate story and journey of humanity, humility, grace, and gratitude, and a passion to contribute to others.

By giving back, and *going back* to the very communities and worlds he had once come from, back to the streets and those he knew needed help most, Tony was determined to live out a life of "paying it backward"—a life of charity and philanthropy that would anchor his days. Amazingly, Tony's personal pledge to himself to a life of giving back began with his earliest days in college and continued on without pause.

Throughout his professional and business career, Tony has led and championed many causes, but especially those within the underprivileged and education communities. From serving for over 10 years as State Chairman of the United Negro College Fund Telethon (Connecticut), to gifting cars annually to families of students with a perfect attendance record, to donating millions of dollars to homeless shelters and rescue missions across America and throughout the world, giving back has been his life.

*Paying It Backward* represents a spirit of philanthropy and charity that speaks to each and every one of us. Almost all of us are in some way connected to hurt and loss, pain and suffering. Following in Tony's footsteps can give you the courage to pay it backward in your world, whatever and wherever that may be.

It has been a special privilege for me to get to know the man the *Tampa Bay Times* referred to as the "Undercover Volunteer." In 2017, a *Times* reporter happened upon a homeless shelter kitchen in Tampa Bay, Florida, where a rather quiet and nondescript older black man had reportedly been serving, incognito, up to 20 hours a week for the past seven years. No one actually knew who that man really was. It was Tony March, the successful car dealership owner.

At a time when our nation and world could use a little inspiration to care more for one another and get back to the values that have always anchored strong communities, Tony's story of "paying it backward" will lift you in so many ways.

~ SEAN COVEY ~

President, Franklin Covey Education

# Life Inside the Black Box

"The hunger for love is much
more difficult to remove than
the hunger for bread."

~ MOTHER TERESA ~

Pain.

Burning, searing, indescribable pain—that's my first memory. I was three years old and, for some reason I'll never know, my mother had waited three years to have me circumcised. With the anesthesia wearing off, I was in agony. I didn't understand what was happening, and I certainly didn't understand why my mother didn't seem to think it was a big deal. I kept looking to her for support, reaching out to her to comfort me and soothe my screams of pain. But that support and comfort never came—not that day or any day since.

The doctors bandaged my wound and sent me home. Over the next week, my mother or older sister casually ripped the bandage off once a day to change the dressing, each time reigniting the fire that sent my three-year-old mind reeling in pain. Days and weeks passed, and the pain eventually subsided. The physical wound healed but left in its place was a psychological wound that never would.

My first memory, my most enduring memory from my childhood, is pain ... and the realization that no one cared.

## — THE GOOD OLD DAYS ... BUT NOT FOR ME —

was born on February 25, 1951, right at the start of the decade many believe was the pinnacle of human civilization. Years earlier, the nation's men had returned home from war and settled down to start families. A decade marked by war and loss had given way to a decade filled with hope. *I Love Lucy* debuted on television that year, giving America a glimpse of the good times and family-friendly values everyone aspired to have in their own homes. "The shot heard 'round the world," a phrase that would have evoked wartime horrors only six years earlier, now described the famous crack of Bobby Thomson's bat as he sent a game-winning, three-run homer flying over the fence at New York's Polo Grounds, cinching the National League pennant for the Giants.

This was set to be a golden decade ... but not for people like me. Like many people of color, my family didn't share in America's golden decade of glory. My focus wasn't on baseball or television; it was on survival. Every day, I woke up scrambling to find food and shelter, fighting prejudice and discrimination, desperately seeking support and affirmation, and struggling to get through life. Welcome to life in the Black Box.

## Born into Poverty

I was one of five children born to my mother, Bertha. I never knew my father and suffered through a long line of my mother's live-in boyfriends and soon-to-be ex-husbands. While I was born in New York, my family moved to Daytona Beach, Florida, when I was very young. We were dirt poor, so housing options were limited. We ended up in a particularly bad part of town called the Black Box, a ghetto mostly filled with other impoverished people of color.

The Black Box was a two-mile block of land literally on the wrong side of the tracks. A rail line separated Daytona's white population from us, and 98 percent of the black community was crammed into this tiny box. Like many public housing projects, the Black Box was overcrowded and underfunded. Row after row of ugly, dilapidated tract-style homes lined each side of the street. Just picture an endless stretch of drab, tiny, and indistinguishable storage units lined up as far as the eye can see. That's what the housing situation looked like in the Box.

My family moved into a 750-square-foot rental unit made up of two small bedrooms, one bathroom, and a living area. Two of my brothers and I shared one bedroom (our older

brother lived with his father), my mother took the other, and my sister Mary, who was nine years older than me, slept on the couch near the front door. We had no heat in the winter, so when the temperature dropped into the thirties, it was cold. The summer was even worse; we had to endure the oppressive Florida heat and humidity without air conditioning. The temperature in the house sometimes exceeded one hundred degrees, and just walking from one room to another left me bathed in sweat.

**In poor communities like ours, people didn't have money for doctors. If you got sick, you toughed it out.**

It sounds bad (because it *was* bad), but it's all I knew back then. With nothing but poverty all around me, I had no idea how desperately poor we were. Everyone else lived like we did, so we never had a concept of any other way of life. If you lived in the Black Box and never went beyond it, you didn't know how people with money lived. I assumed *everyone* lived without air conditioning. How could I miss it when I didn't even know it existed?

Health care was another limited resource in the projects. In poor communities like ours, people didn't have money for doctors. If you got sick, you toughed it out. Or, as a last resort, you went to the hospital emergency room, but that was an option few people considered. In fact, one of my sister's kids died because she waited too long to take him to the hospital. As for me, I was given medical assistance only twice between the ages of four and my high school graduation: once by a dentist, who took care of an abscessed tooth that swelled my jaw to the size of a handball, and once by a physician who treated me for pneumonia. I knew that illness must have been bad, because my mother called a minister to our house and he stayed at my bedside for five hours. I remember wanting to reach out and to thank him, but I didn't have the strength to lift my arm.

And we can't overlook the impact poverty has on something as important as our clothes. For example, I don't remember wearing shoes one time before I started first grade. Kids in the projects *never* wore shoes, especially in the summer. I got my first pair from the Salvation Army when I started school. From then on, I never had more than one pair at a time, and I wore them until they literally fell apart. In fact, I wore them long after holes began eating up the soles. When my shoes got to that point, I had to stuff them with cardboard to plug the holes and get a little more life out of them. Cardboard isn't waterproof, though, so that didn't stop my feet from getting soaked when it rained. To this day, I have fungus on my toenails from walking to and from school in wet shoes. It's a small daily reminder of the life I used to live.

I certainly never got any *new* clothes. Everything I had was either from the Salvation Army, a hand-me-down, or purchased second- or thirdhand for pennies. I didn't get my first truly new piece of clothing until I was sixteen years old, and I had to use my own money for that. I had worked a lot over the summer cutting yards and doing odd jobs. Every dollar I made was precious, so you can imagine how special that first pair of new pants I bought was to me. I remember the feeling of pride I felt as I walked into the first day of eleventh grade wearing my new pants. It's a feeling I'd never had before. It's hard to describe that level of poverty to many people today. You really can't understand unless you've lived it.

## The Thirty-yard Rule and Fifteen-foot Beatings

Living in the ghetto meant safety was always a challenge. Crime was rampant. Switchblades and brass knuckles were readily available, and they were used often. To keep an eye on us and protect us, my mother had a standing rule: no one was allowed to wander more than thirty yards from the front door—where she could see us—unless it involved a specific task she needed done. It felt like my brothers and I were under house arrest whenever we weren't in school or running an errand. Mom meant it, though. If she stepped out the front door and couldn't see me, I'd get a beating. Staying no farther than thirty yards from home meant I had no chance of meeting people and making friends when I was young. So, until I started school, my only playmates were my brothers and the kids who lived next door.

When we were out of sight or out of line, her punishment was hard and swift. By today's standards, my mother probably would've been arrested for child abuse from the beatings she dished out to me and my siblings. We were beaten badly and often, mostly between the ages of three and six. My younger brothers were more mischievous than I was, so they took the brunt of it. I remember cringing in fear when my mother tore into them. I often screamed even though I wasn't the one getting hit, just because I knew just how it felt.

Her instrument of choice was a fifteen-foot-long extension cord, which she used when ironing clothes. When it was time for a whipping, she removed the extension cord from the iron, wrapped part of it around her hand, and used the rest as a whip. It was a cotton-wrapped cord, but it still hurt plenty when it slammed into our backs and butts. That cord left welts all over our backsides and legs even through our pants. And the severity of the beating depended on how mad she was at us. If she was *really* mad, look out! My mother was no lightweight, either. She stood tall at five foot eight—plenty big enough to swing her whip with power.

The beatings were horrible, but there was one bright side with Mom. At least with her, she'd beat you on the spot. During the years we lived with my stepfather, Mom often waited for him to come home so he could get a few lashes in. We routinely got beaten ten hours after we did whatever it was that made her mad. And the fear of waiting for a beating was almost as bad as the beating itself.

Fear was only one of the emotions the beatings brought out in me. As bad as the physical beatings were, I think most of their damage was emotional and psychological. They have had a negative, lifelong impact on me. The trauma of being beaten and watching my brothers get beaten with a fifteen-foot whip made me so severely introverted that I never wanted to come out of my room or do anything with anyone. I was scared that anything—*anything*—could lead to a whipping session. I can still hear my brothers' screams echoing in my head as they pleaded, "Please! Please stop, Mama! I won't do it anymore! I'll be good, I promise!" You just can't shake off those kinds of memories. You feel them in your bones for as long as you live.

I know the trauma of those beatings had a destructive, lifelong effect on me. They contributed to my constant struggles with extreme introversion and bouts of depression. I also believe that abuse is why I so desperately sought affection from my mother. I wanted to be her best child, the kid who always did good things. The son who never needed a beating. Little did I realize that there was *nothing* I could have done to please or impress her. Nothing I've done since then has either.

I view the abuse I suffered as a double-edged sword. On the one hand, it made me depressed and introverted, feeling lousy about myself and not wanting to be around others. On the other, it made me stay in my room and study twice as hard as my peers. Staying in the house like that kept me out of trouble. Plus, studying all those extra hours helped me please my teachers, who appreciated the efforts I made to be a good student.

**I wanted to be her best child, the kid who always did good things. The son who never needed a beating.**

They gave me the affection I so desperately craved and the affirmation my mother could never give. All that studying also helped me achieve the grades I needed to go to college and escape a life of poverty.

There is no excuse or justification for what my mother did

to me. It was a nightmare that I was trapped in throughout my entire childhood, and it was something no child should ever be forced to endure. However, with the benefit of time and therapy, I've been able to extract some good from the bad. Even the most horrible experiences can provide windows of opportunity. If you're facing terrible times right now, don't let those challenges stop you in your pursuit of personal success and happiness. In fact, you can learn to use them as your fire and motivation to push forward. Hopefully I can give you a glimpse of how to do that throughout this book.

— **ALWAYS ON THE MOVE** —

he poverty, substandard housing, and frequent beatings made my life stressful to say the least. Adding to that stress was a total lack of stability. I lived at seventeen different addresses before graduating from high school. Seventeen! That constant sense that I'd have to pack up and move at a moment's notice was traumatic for me. Children *need* some sense of permanence and stability in their lives, but my siblings and I had none at all. The change was nonstop, and we'd sometimes get no more than twenty minutes' notice that it was time to move somewhere else.

The moves were for a variety of different reasons. Sometimes it was financial, and other times my mother would move us into the home of a man she was seeing. Wherever we were, no matter how long we had lived there, we knew a move was coming soon.

It was inevitable. So, it was rarely a surprise when Mom stuck her head in my bedroom door and told me to pack my things. My brothers and I had it down to a science. It took no more than fifteen minutes to pack all our belongings into grocery bags and throw them in the car.

We could move our entire family into a new house in two carloads with the mattresses tied to the roof of the car. We did that a lot.

## Aunt Katie

My favorite place to stay was always at my Aunt Katie's house. We were in and out of her house all the time between moves or when my mother needed a babysitter. Her house was a happy place for me. Aunt Katie had a regular job as a seamstress. She was strong-willed and independent, and she had enough income to feed me when I was with her. That meant so much to me as a child. Up until the time I left for college, Aunt Katie's house was the only place in the world where I didn't have to go to bed hungry.

She was forty-three years older than me and, as time passed, she became the matriarch of our family, lending money to family members when they needed it and taking care of them when they were sick. She even gave one of her houses to my nephew. Although Aunt Katie was generous, she was a tough lady and was not to be taken lightly. Her first husband found that out the hard way.

One night, he tried to break down her door, and she blew him away with a shotgun. Another time, an intruder came up the stairs unannounced, forcing Aunt Katie to use the shotgun once again. Fortunately for him, the blast didn't kill him. Katie's husband hadn't been so lucky. Such was life in the Black Box.

Aunt Katie lived a long, interesting life. She married her final husband at ninety-three years of age and lived with him until he died (of natural causes this time) before passing away herself at 105 years old. She and I grew very close, and she often told me I was her favorite of all her nieces and nephews. Considering the fact that she had *twenty* brothers and sisters and an army of nieces and nephews, that was a huge compliment.

I considered Aunt Katie to be my mother. She was the only adult in my family who gave me not only affection but a sense of my family history. She loved telling stories about our family; about 95 percent of what I know about my genealogy came from her. We often sat down together with her big family Bible, and she'd show me where she recorded the births of everyone in our family, starting with all twenty-one of my grandmother's children. In those days, the Bible always had a place to record your family tree, and Aunt Katie never failed to record a birth in our huge, sprawling family. Aunt Katie would go through that list of names, telling me stories about each of the siblings—when they were born, when they died, and how they lived their lives. She spoke about many of them growing up as sharecroppers on plantations and how poorly they had been treated by their owners.

Learning about my roots with Aunt Katie was precious to me. I could feel a sense of personal history and connection. I heard about their difficulties and I knew I could overcome my own problems. The more time I spent with her, the deeper and more special the bond between us became. When it came time in her later years to appoint a legal guardian, even though her only child was still living, Aunt Katie chose me. One of the saddest times of my life was in 2015, when I arranged the service and burial of the small, selfless powerhouse I considered my true mother.

On her death bed, Aunt Katie made me promise to take care of the family and take up her role as the family leader. It wasn't an easy promise considering everything my family put me through over the years, but it's a responsibility I took on for her. To this day, I work hard at keeping that promise.

### An Orphan Overnight

As much as my Aunt Katie made me feel like a son, my own mother often made me feel like an orphan—sometimes figuratively, but one time all too literally.

We moved so often that I got into a groove. Moving was a huge hassle every time, but I took most of the seventeen moves in stride. Compared to the constant hunger and endless beatings I faced, moving around wasn't that big a deal. One move, though, truly affected me, and it left a lasting feeling of abandonment in my heart and mind.

One morning when I was twelve, my mother woke me, my twin brother, and my younger brother (age eleven) early and said we had to move. She'd already packed our stuff in bags. We all got in the car and Mom started driving us away without telling us where we were going. I could tell this move was different than the others. There was something Mom wasn't telling us.

Finally, once we were on the road with no way to escape, Mom told us the heartbreaking news: she was dropping us off at the local orphanage home. We were stunned and terrified because we'd heard about that place and the kids who lived there. They were looking for someone to take them home, and we always felt sorry for them. Children who weren't adopted were teased by the others, who'd say, "You're too ugly to be adopted" or all kinds of other horrible remarks to make them feel unworthy and unwanted. And now we were going to live among them.

With no warning or real explanation, my mother had decided that my brothers and I were going to be orphans. All she said was, "I need to drop you guys off here for a while because I got some work in New York state. I don't know when I'll be back." That was it. That's all we knew. She got us through the door of the orphanage and disappeared from our lives for three months. Not one time over those months did she ever call, write, or contact us in any way. Even worse, she gave us no indication of when—or even *if*—she would return. We weren't just orphans; we were *unwanted* orphans.

As time passed, I grew more and more terrified that

Mom would never come back and my two brothers and I would be split up by someone adopting one of us and not the others. There were people coming in every day, all day long, interviewing the kids. We knew that children who were there one day might be gone the next. It was like living in an animal shelter. The staff always wanted us to be cute and presentable, saying, "You never know when someone is going to walk in the door and choose you, so you need to be your best at all times." Prospective parents were shown photographs of each child and, if the couple liked what they saw, they'd bring them in to meet the boy or girl. I didn't exactly understand the process, but I knew we didn't want anyone to ask about us. We didn't want to be adopted into another family; we already were a family—broken and abused, but a family, nonetheless.

Every day, I lived with the trauma of worrying I might be separated from my brothers. We were haunted by my mother's words. She said she was coming back for us, but why hadn't we heard from her? When would she return? And would it be too late when she did?

The bright side to our time in the orphanage, though it was hard to call *anything* there a bright side, was the fact that we got to eat three meals a day. However, that benefit was far overshadowed by our fear of being separated—and by having to live such regulated lives. It was a very strict place. They woke us up at 6:00 a.m. every day, and we had to be downstairs for breakfast thirty minutes later. After breakfast, we were assigned chores, like washing dishes or cleaning. Every kid was given a task to keep the orphanage running. After lunch, we could earn some free time, but we always had to stay inside the intimidating chain-link fence that surrounded the orphanage grounds. We had dinner in the evening, after which we had to go directly to our rooms and stay there until the next morning. Nobody was allowed outside their room after dinner except to go to the bathroom. It was like living in a youth prison inside the Black Box.

I talked to a lot of kids in the orphanage. Probably 30 percent of them believed their parents would return and take them home. When those parents didn't show up, the other children would tease them and say, "Forget it. Your parents are never coming back." I always argued that it would be different for me, that my mother would be different. Of course, I had nothing to base that on.

A few times, the stress and fear got the best of me and I went downstairs to see the head of the orphanage, a tough, seemingly heartless woman we called *Mrs. Gestapo*. I asked her when my mother was coming back and she replied bluntly, "I don't know. I haven't heard from her." I asked her over and over again, but she never changed her answer or said anything to reassure me. What other kids said didn't bother me that much; I could take their constant ribbing. But Mrs. Gestapo's complete lack of hope or assurance shook me to the core. Despite the brave face I put on for the other kids, I was worried my mother would never come back and rescue us from the cold, fenced-in land of lost children.

We went to church at the orphanage, and the minister always told us to "keep [our] hope alive." All three of us tried our hardest to follow his advice, believing that Mom would soon return, no matter what the other kids said. But, as time passed, and as we heard nothing from her, our bravado and courage began to fail us. We asked one another, "Why hasn't anyone from the family come to visit us? Where is our sister, Mary? Where is Aunt Katie? Has everyone forgotten about us? Doesn't anyone care?"

If you haven't lived these experiences, you probably can't imagine the hurt of being abandoned by a parent in this way or the fear of being separated from your siblings—not to mention living locked inside the grounds of an orphanage like a prisoner, with no idea what will happen to you. The experience brought us closer together as brothers, but it also showed us how powerless we were at that age to control the world around us.

Then, magically, my mother showed up one day and took us away. She picked us up as though we'd just spent the night at friend's house. No apologies. No explanations. No excuses. If only she had called us when she was gone! If only she had let us know she was coming back, we wouldn't have lived in such fear. But she didn't. She probably never even thought about checking in with us. That was my mother, and that's the way she behaved.

It's been more than fifty years since I spent those three

months in a Black Box orphanage, but I think about those hopeless days and sleepless nights often. As extreme as that experience was, it was just one of many examples of the kind of psychological warfare my mother inflicted upon me growing up. And it's just one of many wounds I've had to live with in the decades since.

## — FIGHTING DYSFUNCTION, ABUSE, AND RACISM —

rowing up poor is tough, even when you've got strong survival instincts. But add in a dysfunctional family life, the lack of a strong father figure, a history of physical and sexual abuse, and, of course, the constant oppression of rampant racism in the 1950s and 1960s (and beyond), and the likelihood of breaking free from poverty and moving into success goes from burdensome to improbable. I'm afraid I had to face all of that and more before I escaped the Black Box.

### The Missing Man

I was a poster child for life in a dysfunctional family environment. My mother gave birth to one daughter, Mary (1942), followed by four sons: Gary (1950), my twin brother Bernard and me (1951), and Gustavo (1952). Despite the full house, I never knew who my real father was. For a while we were told our older brother Gary's father was our dad. But

Gary was the spitting image of him, and we looked nothing alike, so that didn't fit. I remember one day, after hours of playing hopscotch with one of the neighborhood kids, hearing my mother saying, "You know, his father is your real father." But that wasn't true, either. At different points in my childhood, my mother told me three different men were my father. I don't know if she was lying or if she honestly didn't know who my dad was. I guess I'll never know for sure.

To make things more complicated, my mother married and divorced several times. One husband was Ray March, and he was the closest I came to having a father figure in my life. Unfortunately, he wasn't the kind of man who exerted a positive influence on those around him. He wasn't around very much, though, nor did he take care of us when he was. He was a severe alcoholic and got violent when he was drunk. If he didn't come home on Friday with his paycheck, it meant he'd stopped off at a bar on his way home and drank up an entire week's pay. Despite Mom's many failed marriages and string of boyfriends, Ray was the only man I really remember in my mother's life. I guess that's why I ended up with his last name.

One of my last memories of Ray March was when I was eleven, a few days after we moved to a residence on Maple  Street, close to my elementary school. A terrible crash at the front door broke the morning silence. I spun around and saw what looked like an army of FBI agents kicking down our front door. They charged in, slapped handcuffs on Ray, and took him away. Apparently, he'd been stealing other people's mail, forging their signatures, and cashing their checks. He went to prison for a long time, and I didn't see him much after that.

Ray March was not an ideal role model for an eleven-year-old boy. I always kept his name, though. In fact, I always assumed my real, legal name was Anthony March; it's all I ever remembered going by. But when I was seventeen, I was shocked to learn that wasn't my name at all. I had to produce my birth certificate to participate in high school athletics, and it was the first time I'd ever seen the actual document. Imagine my surprise when I saw *someone else's* name on *my* birth certificate! According to the paper, my legal last name was *Reid*, my mother's maiden name. She later told me that when she was admitted into the hospital to give birth to me, she had no idea who my father was, so they put Reid as my last name on my birth certificate. I couldn't believe it, and I refused to go by Reid. Ray March may not have been a great father figure, but I knew I was Tony March. It's who I'd always been, and it's who I'd always be. Six years later, I legally changed my name to March before getting married so my new family would *officially* carry the March family name.

## A Victim of Sexual Abuse

In addition to the poverty, family dysfunction, frequent beatings, and all the other problems lurking in the Black

Box, I also had to face another kind of abuse—the full impact of which I still can't fully evaluate more than sixty years later. Because my mother was essentially on her own, she would sometimes leave us in the care of our sister Mary, who was nine years older than my twin brother and me, or a babysitter from the neighborhood. I was only seven years old the first time that teenage babysitter snuck into my room and sexually abused me. These incidents continued with alarming frequency for three years, until the girl finally moved away.

It's hard to articulate what impact these terrible violations had on me. Casual sex was just a part of life in the Black Box staring at a young age. It was as tied to the projects as poverty—the result of too much time, too many hormone-driven kids living too close together, too few options for other fun activities, and an overall community attitude that didn't discourage children from engaging in adult behavior. My own sister was a prime example. Mary had a total of ten children by the time she turned twenty-five, and the first one was born when she was just fourteen years old. Teenage mothers occupied almost every house down the street. For young people living in squalor and suffering from poverty and abuse, sex was one of the few escapes available. The woods just beyond our row of houses was always full of far-too-young boys and girls getting together.

All that said, what that young woman did to me as a child was not just "casual sex." It wasn't fun or affectionate, and it never made me feel wanted or loved. Rather, it was abuse, plain and simple—just as bad as the beatings I was forced to endure throughout my childhood. I came to expect it with the sense of inevitability that came with growing up poor in a home without love or structure. And, like the beatings, I was not willing to let those sexual violations destroy my will to work hard, overcome the obstacles on my path, and make something of myself.

## Racism: A Partner in Poverty

As I got a little older and hit my teenage years, I took on several odd jobs around town to help support my family and save a little money to buy myself some things my mother couldn't afford. I got part-time jobs in restaurants, cut yards, and did some other jobs that took me to the edge of the Black Box and beyond. Getting outside the Box, though, brought me face to face with new pressures and challenges I hadn't experienced before. The biggest, by far, was the culture of racism that existed in the early 1960s.

Working in this oppressive culture led to one of my most powerful childhood memories—and an odd foreshadowing of my future success. I remember it like it was yesterday. My brothers and I were trying to earn some extra money by selling magazines. We purchased one hundred copies of *Grit* magazine and sold them on street corners for a nickel profit each. Our goal was to make $5 to bring back home to our mother so she could buy food. We did this every Saturday for a while, and we always picked a route with the busiest streets and most potential customers. Our route was two miles long, and we were always dying of thirst from the Florida heat halfway through our sales trek. There was no bottled water back then, but there were plenty of water fountains around. Most of them, though, weren't meant for *people like us.*

There was a car dealership called Lloyd Cadillac and Buick situated right at the halfway point of our route. That's usually where we were at our thirstiest. I can't tell you how many times the dealership employees chased us out of their showroom before my brothers and I could get a quick drink. Even though separate, segregated water fountains and facilities were dying down around the country at that point, the racist attitudes behind them were still very much alive and well. One thing was for sure: the employees on the sales floor at Lloyd Cadillac and Buick certainly didn't want three young, sweaty black boys walking through their showroom. I don't think we ever made it to that water fountain even one time.

Fortunately for us, there was an area behind the dealership where they washed the cars. Willie, the black guy in charge of car-washing, would let us drink from the hose to quench our desperate thirst. While I always appreciated Willie's kindness to us, I also never forgot the frustration I felt as a poor, young black man not being allowed to use the water fountain inside the dealership. It wasn't just humiliating; it was outright degrading. The people there made me feel less-than-human, like my life wasn't worth even a sip of water. I never forgot the feeling of being forced to drink out of a dirty hose out of sight of the "civilized" people. Little did I know then that I'd have a much different encounter with Lloyd Cadillac and Buick thirty-five years later. But that's a story for another chapter.

## — ENDLESS HUNGER —

unger has been one of the most powerful forces in my life. I was hungry all the time, every single day, right up until I went to college. Overcoming hunger was one of my biggest challenges and motivations in surviving as a child, and today, memories of that terrible hunger fuel my passion to provide food for others.

### The Never-ending Struggle

The feeling of hunger never goes away. You go through the actions of your day, but your empty belly growls all the way through, and the thought of food consumes you. It was a never-ending struggle in our household, and there were reminders everywhere that I was hungry. In school, we had a fruit break in the afternoon, so parents would send along an apple or orange for their kids to eat in class. We couldn't afford anything like that, so I couldn't participate. I just had to sit there while all the other kids ate their fruit.

Government aid often provided some staples like powdered eggs, sugar, rice, flour, cheese, butter, and maybe a can of Spam, but it was sporadic. Weeks could pass with no aid at all. During those times, the entire family shared one dollar's worth of groceries per day: a box of grits, a bag of beans, and a bag of rice. On rare occasions, when Mom brought in some extra income as a hairdresser, we could buy meat from the butcher. He sold everything to the black community that the white people didn't want to eat—oxtails, neck bones, the head and feet of pigs, even the guts. It may not sound like a feast to you, but it was fine dining for poor black families who'd spent all week eating nothing but rice and beans.

**He sold everything to the black community that the white people didn't want to eat ...**

Scraping by on a bare-bones diet, we were always on the lookout for something to supplement what we had. Sometimes, in the name of survival, we made inventive, unorthodox, and even unsettling choices—like canal fishing. There was a canal near our neighborhood, and my mother often piled all of us into the car and made us sit there while she fished for five or six hours. She used a bamboo pole and worms she harvested from our backyard compost heap. The fish were only about the size of my hand, but we were always excited when she was successful. We ate every part too: the head, the eyes, the works. I learned how to slit a fish and take out the insides, and then

Mom would deep-fry what was left in a big black skillet. She used lard to fry it up, and she kept whatever grease was left in a coffee can. She pulled out that can of lard every time she cooked, to the point that the food always tasted burnt. It was probably the most unhealthy, saturated fat on earth. I can still taste it now.

## Stolen Sweets and Winn-Dixie Wednesdays

My brothers and I sometimes went to extreme measures to get something into our bellies. One time when I was five years old, I smelled the most intoxicating, heavenly aroma of my life floating over from next door. Our neighbor had just baked a pineapple upside-down cake. She had left her back door open, which seemed crazy to me. Why on earth would she want all that sweet-smelling perfection to escape? Once that scent hit our empty kitchen, my brothers and I lost all our senses. We were drawn to the neighbor's house like ants to a pile of sugar. It was just automatic, like I wasn't in control of my body. We snuck through her open door, crept into her kitchen, and wolfed down all but one tiny slice. We would have eaten it too, but the neighbor caught us in our final moments of gluttony. When she told my mother about what we'd done, we received one of the worst beatings of our lives. It was worth it, though. To this day, pineapple upside-down cake remains my all-time favorite dessert. Nothing else comes close.

The beating we got didn't stop my brothers and me

from foraging for food; it just changed where we looked. Rather than sneaking into neighbors' kitchens, for example, we picked through their garbage cans. I was a full-fledged dumpster diver by the age of seven. One day, I was going through the trash of a lady who lived three doors down from us and found the discarded remains of a chocolate cake. Chocolate cake! I hit the jackpot! I didn't hesitate. I reached down, pulled what was left of the cake out of the trash, carefully scraped off the mold, waved away the flies, and picked off the maggots. Once it appeared mold- and maggot-free, I stuffed the whole thing in my mouth and enjoyed the rare treat. What a great day!

The glory of the day's discovery didn't last, however. A short while later, I developed severe stomach cramps and had...well, problematic bathroom experiences. It became clear that I had gotten tapeworms from my garbage cake. The flies and maggots should have been a giveaway, I guess. Of course, we never went to the doctor for this. Instead, my mother treated the condition by making me drink beer. It must have worked, because everything cleared up soon afterward. Besides, there's no way my mother would have wasted a beer on me if she wasn't sure it'd work.

The peak of our dumpster-diving days hit when we moved close to a Winn-Dixie supermarket when I was ten years old. The dumpsters they kept behind the store were a gold mine. My brothers and I quickly figured out that Wednesday evenings were the best times to strike. The store refreshed their produce department every Wednesday, and every vegetable and piece of fruit that didn't look fresh was thrown out along with the old bread. What they saw as garbage, we saw as an absolute bonanza!

We couldn't believe what they just tossed aside as trash. The best thing was the corn. Who cared if the top half was brown? The bottom half was good, so we just tossed the bad half away. The same was true with bananas and tomatoes; we'd throw out the rotten part and keep the good stuff. Carrots were particularly good; they lasted a long time before they spoiled. Good apples were harder to find, but even the rottenest apple had at least one or two good bites left on it.

I understand if this all sounds disgusting to you, but nothing made us happier than finding a pile of half-rotten fruit in a grocery-store dumpster. You have to view it through the lens of poverty. When you're starving and haven't had a good meal in days or weeks, picking through someone's trash to find a good carrot makes all the sense in the world. A truly hungry person will do just about anything to get something to eat, and dumpsters are usually full of food that's still edible, free, and easy to grab. It was perfectly normal to us. In fact, our mother knew we were bringing home food from the dumpster. My brothers and I would eat the good parts of the bananas and other fruit before we got home and give the rest to Mom to use in the meager meals she made. This went on for several years until we moved too far from the Winn–Dixie to continue "shopping" there.

My dumpster-diving days came to an end at around age twelve. The pickings had gotten too slim since we moved away from the Winn–Dixie, and I decided I could live without the tapeworms . . . and the beer.

## A Krispy Kreme Commitment

My obsession with food only got worse as I entered my teen years, hit a growth spurt, and began playing multiple sports in high school. Our weekly Winn–Dixie trip was gone, and the meal portions we got from home were hardly sufficient. I was living with my sister, Mary, and her husband at that point, and she had nine kids of her own to feed. There just wasn't enough to go around for all twelve of us. I was so intensely hungry every single day.

Things came to a head one morning when I was walking to school. I carried my entire food supply for the day, a single sandwich . . . if you could call it that. It was actually two slices of bread with a thin layer of grape jelly spread so thin that it barely created a sheen on the bread's surface. Not only did this sandwich have to suffice as my entire lunch, but it had to sustain me through a grueling after-school wrestling session that lasted for hours and burned a huge number of calories. Making it through the day fueled by this one, thin grape sandwich would have been difficult enough. The donut shop I had to pass on the way to school, though, put the whole thing over the top.

I will never forget this experience for as long as I live. I can still see, hear, and smell everything just as it was at 7:45 that morning in eleventh grade. My walk to school sent me past a Krispy Kreme donut shop. The owner was a clever guy; he made sure to vent the scent of the freshly baked donuts out to the street to draw in passersby. I have only ever had a Krispy Kreme twice in my life, but I can remember every detail of how they taste and smell. When I got to the corner of Madison and Volusia that morning, I walked right through a cloud of intoxicating donut heaven. I only *thought* I was hungry before. Once the smell of those donuts hit me, my hunger went out of control. I kept telling myself to put it out of my mind, to ignore the hunger and save my sandwich for lunch. I knew it'd be next to impossible to get through the next twelve hours with nothing to eat and that my little sandwich—as thin and meager as it was—was all I had to get me through my afternoon classes and wrestling practice. I kept telling myself all these things, but it ultimately didn't matter. I was so out of my mind with hunger that I tore into my lunch bag and devoured my little grape sandwich right there on the street.

When the sandwich was gone, barely having made a dent in my hunger, I broke down and cried. I cried harder than I'd ever cried before. It was a life-defining moment for me. I made a commitment right there on the street corner next to Krispy Kreme to change my life and my future. I said to myself, *I will not live the rest of my life in poverty. No matter what it takes, I will get out of here and be a success.* That's a commitment I've looked back on often throughout my life.

I somehow made it through the rest of the school day and wrestling practice, powered by nothing but sheer force of will. I've also kept the promise I made to myself that day. But I will never forget that feeling of hunger ... or the helplessness that came with it.

## — GETTING OVER MY MOTHER —

This has been a hard chapter. It was hard for me to write, and I'm willing to bet it's been hard for you to read. Surviving inside the Black Box was all-out warfare every single day. I fought through poverty, hunger, prejudice, beatings, family dysfunction, sexual abuse, abandonment, constant relocations, loneliness, isolation, and more. It never stopped. As bad as all these things were, though, they weren't responsible for most of the stress and anxiety I felt back then, and they aren't responsible for the lingering emotional wounds I still carry with me today. No, the root cause of most of my *real* problems then and now was actually the one person who was *supposed* to love and support me through all of it: my mother.

I've said many things about my mother already, but allow me to properly introduce her and talk about what it was like having her for a mom. Bertha Reid was born in Tallahassee, Florida, in 1926. She came from a large family and was the youngest of twenty-one. By the time she became a mother herself, she had already developed a child-rearing philosophy shaped by her own hardships and dysfunctional relationships with men. The result of her struggles was a complete inability to show affection to her children. She was, by all outward appearances, numb to the fact that she had five little kids who depended on her. I believe it was this lack of motherly instinct that caused me the most damage and left a permanent scar on my psyche.

I really don't know anything about my mother's life before I was born. I know nothing of her childhood or how she grew up. I don't know how she got to New York. I just know I was born there, and a couple of months later, she moved us to Daytona Beach, where she worked as a beautician. She occasionally worked at beauty shops, and I can remember sitting in her car all day long while she worked her shift. She'd also cut hair on the side, and many of my childhood memories are of black women, one at a time, getting their hair done in our kitchen sink.

What I remember most about my mother was her unwillingness, her *inability,* to give me the affection I was so desperate for. I wanted so badly to feel loved and appreciated. I tried to behave not just to avoid the beatings but to earn her affection. But I never could. I can remember every detail of all those beatings—dozens of them—but I can't recall a single time when she hugged me. She didn't even get up close to spank us, preferring to beat us from a distance using her fifteen-foot extension-cord whip instead.

Mom never read a single sentence of a book to me—not one bedtime story—and she certainly didn't have any interest in playing with me. Of course, dropping us off at an orphanage and leaving us there for months with no word or hope for her return didn't win her any points. Neither did her gifting practices for birthdays and Christmas. I didn't experience a birthday party until I was twelve years old. Of course, Christmas presents were a rare commodity in our household too. Sure, we were poor, but so were our neighbors. Yet, on Christmas Day, we'd go outside and see the other kids on new roller skates and playing with new toys. It was a terrible feeling knowing that my mother didn't care enough to buy us a single gift for Christmas morning.

> **On Christmas Day, we'd go outside and see the other kids on new roller skates and playing with new toys.**

One Christmas Eve when I was twelve, my mother made us stay home all day. When she finally walked in the door, she was carrying several bags. My brothers and I got all excited thinking, at last, we might get some presents. Well, the next morning I *did* get a gift. It was a textbook three inches thick that was more suited to a college senior in a humanities class than a twelve-year-old boy. It probably cost her twenty cents.

What was in the other bags? Two six-packs of beer.

I was so disappointed, but more than that, I knew this was inappropriate behavior for a parent. If I were a parent, I would have taken the money she spent on that beer and bought gifts for my kids. To this day, that twelfth Christmas remains the worst of my life, and Christmas Day is emotionally the worst day of the year for me. I just can't shake it.

As I'll discuss in the next chapter, I always brought home good report cards, hoping for some word of congratulations or encouragement. But Mom never acknowledged my achievements; there were no compliments or pats on the back. She was wholly indifferent to my accomplishments. I wanted her to appreciate me, to show me some warmth, and I thought maybe academic success was the way...but she just didn't seem to care.

The number one void in my life as a child was the lack of affection. Not the hunger, not the abuse, not the crazy instability of our lives. It was the fact that I didn't feel loved. It makes me so sad to think about. Today, my mother is still alive and lives only two hours away. However, I haven't seen her since 2000, and I probably won't see her again for the rest of her life. I just don't think any peace or resolution would come of seeing her again.

I've worked for a long time to understand my mother's behavior and, after years of therapy, I have a few ways of coping. In 2006, in a bout of severe depression, a psychologist named Arthur taught me to "take my mother and all those memories and put her in the cabinet above the refrigerator." For some reason, that worked, and it still helps me when memories of abuse threaten to overtake me.

Every Sunday as a child, my mother dragged us to the church of whatever religion she believed in at the time. Those services were hard to sit through, and I took such care to not move a muscle out of fear of a beating when we got home. Still, those Sunday sermons planted a seed of faith in my life that has blossomed into a wonderful relationship with God. As crazy as it sounds under the circumstances, I have to thank Mom for bringing God into my life. It's one of the only gifts she ever gave me.

As I've grown older and built a better relationship with God, I have often asked for His help in forgiving my mother. I return, again and again, to the idea that maybe she was never taught to love. Maybe she, too, was the victim of abuse, isolation, alcoholism, and dysfunction. I'll never know for sure, but I think that's probably true. At least that's the reason I've created to excuse her terrible behavior...so I can heal.

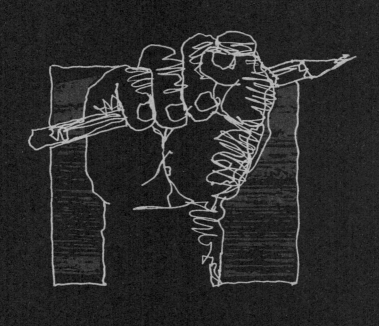

# TWO

# Education: My Great Escape

"Ask any successful person, and most will tell you
that they had a person who believed in them...
a teacher, a friend, a parent, a guardian, a sister,
a grandmother. It only takes one person,
and it doesn't really matter who it is."

~ SEAN COVEY ~

was excited about starting first grade. We lived
across the street from a school, and I often watched
the kids playing. The thought of making new
friends was exciting, as was the prospect of being away
from home and the constant monitoring of my mother and
older sister. I also heard that food was served, which would
be a big deal to me. And, of course, there was the prospect
of learning new things. I'd always been an innately curious
child, and I desperately wanted to know more about the
world that stretched beyond the thirty-yard boundary
around our house. I had the biggest smile on my face that
first day of class. Little did I know, things were only going
to get better.

## — SETTLING INTO SCHOOL —

or the first nine years of my schooling, I attended schools with predominately black students. Even though the Supreme Court had declared school segregation illegal a few years earlier in 1954, many states like Florida had yet to fully implement the judicial ruling. That didn't bother me; I was just excited to get out of the house every day!

### Surrogate Mothers

Even though I was a cautious introvert and already showing psychological distress as a result of my upbringing, the classroom environment seemed to open me up. Whippings were the favored mode of interaction for Bertha Reid with her children, but at school, my good behavior was recognized by my teachers and I was praised for it. It was an awakening: the appreciation I desperately needed and was denied at home was in ample supply at school. My teachers were quick to encourage me and compliment my achievements, and this drove me to do my very best. It was an upward spiral of success: the harder I worked, the more attention and praise I received; the more attention and praise I received, the harder I worked.

At the end of that first grading period, I brought home a report card with straight As. Finally, I had *documented proof* that I'd done a good job at something. I couldn't wait to show my mother! I should have known better. She showed little to no interest in my achievement. It was a bitter disappointment; I still remember the pain of that first report card six decades later. All I could do from that point on was bury my hurt and disappointment and turn to my teachers for the affection, encouragement, and positive attention I never received at home. I tried not to think about impressing my mother and instead focused on impressing my teachers. I wanted to get straight As every time to show them I was a good student so they'd keep feeding me the encouragement and pats on the back that I desperately needed. Those incredible ladies became my surrogate mothers. I came to rely on my teachers' unflinching love and support all the way through school, right up to my high school graduation. I honestly don't think I could have made it without each of them. I owe them the world.

## A Knack for Math

Looking back over those first few years of school, I can see how I managed to squeeze some good out of my mother's strict rules, my need for my teachers' affirmation, and my natural introversion. While other kids were outside playing, making new friends, and venturing more than thirty yards from their homes, I was hiding out in my room studying. I'd estimate that I spent fifty percent more time studying than my fellow classmates, and that started to pay off in a big way.

By the time I hit third grade, I realized I had a natural gift for mathematics. Our class was learning the multiplication tables, and I mastered everything up to 12x12 within two weeks. The rest of the class was still struggling with 2x2! It was the first time I can remember feeling smart. It wasn't long before I was two to three years ahead of the other students in my math classes.

As I progressed through school, I discovered that my innate talents in math also included the sciences. I loved those classes! Everything didn't come that easily to me, though. My Achilles' heel, I quickly discovered, was English. I guess this makes sense, considering the fact that my mother never once read me a story or put any value at all in the written word.

> **I walked past my daughter's bedroom and overheard my wife reading Snow White and the Seven Dwarfs to her. I'd never heard of it.**

Despite a houseful of five children, I don't think there was a single children's book in our home growing up. This point was driven home for me much later in life, after I was married and had a child of my own. I walked past my daughter's bedroom and overheard my wife reading *Snow White and the Seven Dwarfs* to her. I'd never heard of it. Imagine a grown man in his thirties having to look up "Snow White"—a nearly two-hundred-year-old fairy tale that every child (except me) knew well. This experience really bothered me. I loved hearing my wife's voice reading my child to sleep, but I came away feeling somber and depressed. I realized that *this* is what normal parents do for their children, but my mother couldn't even do *this much*.

## — FLYING WITH THE HAWKS —

continued to excel in math and science (and struggle with English) as I moved through elementary and middle school. Then came eighth and ninth grade, two years that marked a critical turning point in my academic studies and set me up for the educational journey I would take after high school. This was also when my "HAWKs" appeared on the scene. Later in life, I gave that acronym to four special teachers—Mrs. Harris, Mrs. Aumiller, Mrs. West, and Mrs. Keyes—who took me under their wings and gave me the opportunity and encouragement I needed to soar on my own. Their praise and support helped me rise above the sadness and see the potential in my life. They made me feel worthwhile and wanted, giving me the applause and appreciation that propelled me to greater heights. Their faith in me made my personal success and my life in service to others possible. I am blessed to have had them in my life.

If anyone has any doubt about the essential, influential role teachers play in the lives of our children, I'd encourage them to take a look at the impact the HAWKs had on my life. I truly believe the best way to break the cycle of poverty is education. I wouldn't be where I am today without these incredible teachers. Let me tell you about them and how they helped me navigate grades eight through twelve.

## The First HAWK: Mrs. Keyes

I met my first HAWK, Mrs. Keyes, in eighth grade. She was
my math teacher for grades eight and nine. Like all great
teachers, Mrs. Keyes knew all students have their own unique
abilities, and she quickly saw that I had a real aptitude for math.
I raised my hand so often to answer her questions in class that
she stopped calling on me to ensure the other students had
a chance to participate. Because I was in an all-black school,
which was always underfunded, there were no honors classes
or advanced learning programs available, but Mrs. Keyes
improvised and came up with the next best thing. She gave me
my own curriculum to follow and provided advanced math
texts for me so I could learn at my own pace as I sat at the back
of the classroom.

From first through ninth grade, I racked up straight As
in every subject I took, except for English, where I had to
settle for Cs. Of all the As I got, it was one test in particular
in Mrs. Keyes' class that made the biggest impression on me.
She handed my test paper back to me and I saw that she'd
written "A+++" across the top. When I looked up at her,
though, I could tell she was mad. I didn't understand. Why
did she look so angry if I had done so well on the test? Later,
she explained that she often got mad at seeing so many black
kids with so much potential completely squander their gifts and
opportunities. Mrs. Keyes didn't want that to be my story. She
took me aside and said, "Tony, if I ever see you on the back of a
garbage truck, I'm going to stop my car, pull you off, and beat
your behind. You're too good for that. Don't let your talent go

to waste!" It was the first time anyone had ever told me I was "too good" for anything. And, it was the first time I let myself start dreaming of a life outside the Black Box. It was a life-defining moment for me.

Mrs. Keyes didn't stop there, though. She was determined to give me the best possible chance at succeeding. That involved getting me into the right high school. Now, I *should* have gone directly from my predominantly black middle school to Campbell High School, the mostly black high school where all my classmates would end up. But Mrs. Keyes knew I would be more challenged and receive a better education at Mainland High School, a mostly white school. Mainland had superior facilities, more advanced courses, better-trained teachers, and higher standards than Campbell could provide.

She went directly to the central administration decision-makers and, based on my record, petitioned that I be allowed to attend Mainland. She was successful in her efforts, but I was still required to *apply* to attend Mainland. It was a public high school but, because I was black, I had to petition to get in. Remember, segregation was still a way of life in our schools then, even though the Supreme Court had already ruled against it. Ultimately, I was accepted, but I did end up with some culture shock. I went from a school that was almost exclusively black to a facility with two thousand students and all but eight of them were white!

Not only did she get me into a superior high school,

but Mrs. Keyes was one of the main reasons I later chose
to enter engineering school. She taught me the advanced
math I needed to qualify for the program and succeed once
I got there.

## Life at Mainland

Things were looking up for me as I began classes at
Mainland. The academic demands were a lot tougher than
they had been at Campbell but, thanks to the teaching and
tenacity of Mrs. Keyes, I was well-prepared to succeed in
the more demanding learning environment. Something
unexpected happened a few weeks into the semester,
though: my mother packed everyone up, gave her house to
my sister, and moved to Miami to open her own hair salon.
Of course, she never even considered what that meant for
my education now that I was in one of the best schools
around. I initially moved to Miami with her (mainly out
of habit), but soon realized I'd much rather be back in
Daytona Beach attending Mainland. Fortunately, my sister
agreed to let me live with her family in Mom's old house,
so I moved in with Mary, her husband, and their nine
children. Needless to say, things were much more crowded
than they were before, but I was happy to be back at my
new school.

   Life at Mainland took some getting used to. The
courses were more demanding and the students far better
prepared than my classmates back at Campbell. I suddenly

found myself among peers who shared my mathematical skills and were serious about their studies. What could I do to stay on top? Well, I took my study efforts up another notch. I didn't date. I didn't talk on the phone. I didn't watch television when I got home. Except for participating in athletics and the school band, I lived a monastic life of classes and hour upon hour of homework. Every day was the same: wake up, go to school, attend sports practice, return home, study, go to bed. Rinse and repeat day after day after day. I never even stayed up past 11:00 p.m. until the night of my high school graduation. I was definitely a geek by today's standards...and I was totally fine with that. If that's what it took to become successful and get out of this life of poverty once and for all, so be it.

Sadly, staying ahead of the game academically wasn't my only challenge at Mainland. I also had to deal with the very raw reality of racism, both in town and in school. My first year at Mainland was 1966, and racism was rampant. You might find this hard to believe, but at the time, there were still a few segregated bathrooms in Daytona with "Colored" signs on them. A black person expected harassment at many diners and restaurants—unless he was in the company of some white friends. That was rare, though. There was significant cultural pressure to keep the races separate. Any white person who hung out with black friends would routinely be

**At the time, there were still a few segregated bathrooms in Daytona with "Colored" signs on them.**

called a "n----- lover." And a black guy dating a white girl? Forget it.

As one of only eight black students at Mainland, I faced racism and prejudice everywhere I turned. Because I was a pretty good athlete, I had an easier time getting along with my white classmates than others, but it definitely wasn't a free pass. I remember one time my senior year when I was walking to school in a heavy downpour. As I waited to cross the street, a pretty white girl in a shiny new car pulled up, waiting for the light to change. She looked over at me and we recognized each other, as we were both Mainland students. Here I was, getting completely drenched, and she just looked me in the eye and drove off when the light turned green. I tried to rationalize her actions by empathizing with her. I understood she couldn't drive up to school and have a black guy get out of her car. But I will never forget that day.

Playing sports as a black athlete at a white school had its own unique set of advantages and disadvantages. The best part was enjoying a safe haven—or at least a reprieve—from segregation. While I was with my team and practicing, coaches and teammates weren't saying "Hey, n-----, make that tackle." They were saying, "*Tony*, make that tackle." But then, during a football game, players on the opposing team would try to get me riled up by calling me the N-word. I've always believed in fighting racism by taking the high road, so if a guy called me that, I'd get back at him on the field, not by arguing with him. Besides, in those days, we couldn't vocally express our dislike for someone who was taunting us with disparaging, racist terms. We'd get beaten ... or worse. Some black kids just couldn't take it and they let their frustrations get the best of them. And what happened? They got kicked off the team. So, I had to walk on eggshells all the time if I wanted to stay on the team and stay in the school that was helping me get where I wanted to go.

On top of the challenging academics and constantly dealing with prejudice, I also had to deal with the never-ending reality of poverty during those years. It was a relentless drain—psychologically and physiologically—on my capacity to function at full potential. I could barely find enough food to keep my teenaged stomach filled and my strength intact. It was a wonder that I managed to excel in three sports while on such a starvation diet. But it didn't stop me from winning a regional title in wrestling. In fact, I guess I could say it helped because that constant state of hunger kept me in the weight class in which I won my title.

My lack of financial resources also deprived me of the extracurricular activities most students took for granted. I was resigned to missing all the field trips planned for my class. I didn't have the chance to attend my junior or senior proms, either, because I couldn't afford to rent a tuxedo. Walking around in shoes with holes in them and carefully mending my clothes as they fell apart ... my clothing budget was just like my caloric intake: next to nothing. These were all painful, constant reminders that I was an outsider at Mainland, that my classmates could never understand the life I was living or the price I was paying just to be there with them.

There was one big event that really puts my poverty struggle in perspective. My junior year, I played trombone in the high school band. Students had to purchase their own instruments back then, so I had used $15 of that summer's hard-earned yard-cutting money to buy an old trombone from a pawn shop. It wasn't great, but it got the job done. That fall, our band was one of only two high school bands chosen to represent Florida in that year's Macy's Thanksgiving Day Parade. Thanks to various fundraising activities, the band was able to accept the invitation. This was my first chance ever to travel out of state. But, just a month before the scheduled Macy's march, my trombone broke. The slide didn't function anymore, and you can't play a trombone without a slide. I didn't have the money to fix it, but there was no way I was going to miss that trip.

I marched in that Macy's Thanksgiving Day Parade with holes in my shoes and a trombone that wouldn't play. I faked every song, extending my arms dramatically to look like I was playing in sync with the others, but there was no sound at all coming out of my instrument. Everyone else was playing their hearts out with great gusto while I could only pretend to play. The band leader knew it, too, but he never said a word. He let me fake my performance so I wouldn't miss the trip. It was such a small kindness, but it's one I will always remember.

To top it all off, I had no money to buy souvenirs. My bandmates' parents had given them money so they could purchase a few things to remind them of this incredible adventure. But a poor kid from the Black Box with holes in his soles and a broken trombone just couldn't afford any trinkets from New York. Business as usual, I guess.

## The Second HAWK: Mrs. Aumiller

By eleventh grade, I was well into my predictable routine of long days of classes, sports practice and hours of homework. I didn't have a social life, and that suited me just fine. I had figured out the formula that got me the affection and attention I needed, and nothing was going to pull me off course.

That year, a new HAWK arrived in my life when I was placed in Mrs. Aumiller's Chemistry 2 class. As always, I was committed to making a great impression by exceeding her expectations. When I did well, she smiled at me. I could live off that feeling for days. The high point of my time with Mrs. Aumiller was the day she gave the class a particularly tough test, our final exam. She told us beforehand that she was going to award small prizes to the three students who earned the highest test score. The prizes were small, but the bragging rights were huge. The smartest kids in school were in that class with me, and we *all* wanted to be recognized as one of the "top three." Pride was on the line, and respect was waiting for the winners.

Mrs. Aumiller announced the test results, building up the suspense by starting with the third-place finisher. That honor went to a girl who was my class nemesis, a student who was always trying to outdo me. Second place was awarded to a guy I hardly knew. At that point, I felt a surge of disappointment and thought, *I didn't even make the top three? I thought I nailed that test.* Then Mrs. Aumiller began to tear up. She paused dramatically and then a huge smile lit up her face as she announced, "The winner who earned the highest score is Tony March!"

The way she said it, it was as though I was her own child. I could *feel* how proud she was of me, and that's what it was all about: earning that expression on a teacher's face that I should have received from a loving parent. I knew nobody in my own family would care enough to congratulate me for my performance on that test, but that was okay as long as I earned my teacher's applause. Mrs. Aumiller's reaction was the perfect example of why I saw the HAWKs as my surrogate mothers. I would do anything to receive their praise.

**Second place was awarded to a guy I hardly knew. At that point, I felt a surge of disappointment and thought, *I didn't even make the top three?***

I had Mrs. Aumiller as my chemistry teacher for two years—in both eleventh and twelfth grade—and she got me more excited about a career in the sciences than anyone else ever had. That interest and investment came to a head when she encouraged me to participate in Florida's statewide science fair. Every year, students from across the state submitted pioneering and imaginative projects to a panel of judges. These weren't the basic, rudimentary projects you can find in most school-level science fairs. No, these were *serious* scientific studies by incredibly gifted young scientists and budding engineers. With Mrs. Aumiller's encouragement, I threw my hat in the ring and registered for the science fair—along with literally two hundred and fifty *thousand* other Florida students.

After spending some time thinking through possible topics and reading several books for inspiration, I finally told Mrs. Aumiller, "I think I'll focus on the semimicro determination of carbons and hydrogens in organic material." She said it sounded more like a college level thesis, but she gave me the go-ahead, anyway. More importantly, she gave me her support. Knowing I didn't have the financial means to pay for materials, she purchased my supplies with her own money. And that wasn't all. She gave me a key to her classroom so I could work on the project during the summer. Every summer day for two years, I went to school, let myself into her classroom, and built my project. If I needed more parts, she'd buy them. When I needed parts of the report typed up, she did that for me too. She was right there with me every step of the way.

For my project, I built a machine that would burn an object and pass its fumes through filters. I could then weigh the material in the filters and use a math formula to determine how much hydrogen and carbon was in each object. My first subject was a cockroach. By sacrificing the pest to science, I was able to figure out exactly how much of a roach's body was made up of carbon and hydrogen.

By the time I'd finished building my machine, it was so large it didn't fit in the classroom. Mrs. Aumiller made arrangements for me to use a room in the junior college nearby. The next issue was a lack of transportation; I had no way to get to the junior college to work on my project. She solved that problem, too, with her new, cherry-red Mustang convertible. During a time when prejudice and racism were running rampant, this bold teacher drove me across town in her convertible to and from the junior college every day. She was determined to help me complete my work.

One day, she had a meeting and couldn't take me to the junior college. I thought I'd just lose the day of work, but she shocked me by saying, "Here are my keys. You can drive over there yourself." Can you imagine how I felt in that moment? I had never experienced such a display of trust and faith in my life. She probably assumed I had my driver's license, but I had never actually driven on a street in my life. There I was, a black teenager in the 1960s South driving a bright red convertible all by myself. You better believe I drove carefully and did everything I could to keep her car safe!

Throughout those two years of working on my project, Mrs. Aumiller—a white teacher in a white school—gave me the keys to her classroom and the keys to her car. If anything had happened, she could have been fired ... or worse. Knowing she was in my corner, encouraging me every step of the way, gave me the courage to keep pressing on, even though I was going up against half a million other bright students. That April, Mrs. Aumiller arranged for me to present my project to the panel of five judges in Jacksonville. She even set up the transportation to get me and my massive machine there, and she stood by me as I had explained my project in detail to the judges.

After reviewing all the entries, the judges awarded the "Prize of Excellence" to the ten most impressive projects in the state. I couldn't believe it when they chose my project as one of the winners. It wasn't just another piece of evidence that I was actually gifted in math and science; it was proof that Mrs. Aumiller's time, trust, encouragement, and sacrifice were worth it. I'm not sure which one of us was prouder of my award! I do know, however, that there's no way I would have won that science fair without Mrs. Aumiller. As proud as I was to win, I'm sad to say this was another time when my family's complete lack of attention became painfully evident. Neither my mother nor any other family member came to see me win this prestigious award, and a new wave of deep depression washed over me for a while.

Decades later, after I'd achieved success that *that* "young Tony" never would've believed, I ran into Mrs. Aumiller on the dance floor at my high school reunion. We hugged and cried for a good ten minutes with people bumping into us as they danced.

## The Third HAWK: Mrs. West

I met my third HAWK in my senior year at Mainland.
Mrs. West did more to prepare me for college than anyone,
fueling my appetite for higher learning and helping me
develop the sense of self-worth I'd need to achieve my
success goals. She taught a "super honors" math class for
only the twelve brightest math students in the school. This
was the most advanced course at Mainland, and Mrs. West
allowed me to join it.

Throughout that year, Mrs. West taught me
fundamental math tricks I could perform in my head that
helped hone my quantitative skills. She inspired me, talking
about the science of math and its real-world applications
in problem-solving. She prepared me for college, too, by
focusing on SAT prep. Because of her teaching, I managed
to get one of the highest scores in the entire school on the
SAT math exam, which was a critical piece of my eventual
college acceptance. I appreciated Mrs. West and the other
HAWKs even more when I finally got to college, because
my first year of classes were a piece of cake after all the hard
coursework Mrs. West, Mrs. Aumiller, and Mrs. Keyes put
me through.

## The Fourth HAWK: Mrs. Harris

Even though I nailed the math portion of the SAT and had
excelled in Mainland's hardest college-level courses, I had
never given much thought to going to college. It just wasn't

in the cards for most kids from the Black Box. I couldn't afford it, of course, and I had also bombed the English portion of the SAT with a dismal 325 score. Those two factors seemed like insurmountable obstacles, a huge wall standing between me and higher education.

Enter Mrs. Harris, my fourth HAWK. She was the guidance counselor at Mainland High School. As such, she knew all about my scholastic achievements, science fair award, straight As in the most advanced math and science classes, and my high SAT math score. She was also aware of my financial situation and the low English score on the college entrance exam. When I went in to meet with her about my future plans—a requirement for all Mainland seniors—I told her I wasn't planning on attending college. Knowing my school record, Mrs. Harris just shook her head and said, "No, Tony. We've *got* to get you into college. With all you've done and all you're capable of, I know without a doubt that you'd excel at college-level work."

**Mrs. Harris just shook her head and said, "No, Tony. We've got to get you into college."**

## A Chance Encounter Changes My Life

You know the old adage about being in the right place at the right time? It was March of my senior year, 1969, and I had not even applied to any college. Not long after my chat with Mrs. Harris, I got home to my sister's house after a full day of class and sports practice to find her sitting in the living room talking to a man I didn't know. She introduced me to Moses Johnson, her husband's best friend. He'd had a business trip nearby and wanted to stop by for a visit before going back home. Moses explained that he was the dean of Admissions for Howard University, a highly respected college in Washington, D.C., known for some prestigious alumni, which included several of the most successful black men and women in America. I was, of course, familiar with the university and was stunned to find one of its key administrators standing in our little living room in the Daytona projects.

Before I walked in, my sister, Mary, had already told Moses all about my academic success. That in itself was surprising, as my family had never paid any attention to my achievements at school. Moses, though, was intrigued. He asked me all about the advanced courses I was taking and was surprised when I mentioned Chemistry 2, Physics 2, and Calculus. When I nervously told him about my high math SAT score, he didn't try to hide his excitement.

Moses asked me where I was going to attend college. I told him I wasn't going anywhere because I couldn't afford it. He said, "But you've *already* completed courses that Howard students haven't even taken yet! There's no way you're not going to college! When I get back to my office on Monday, I'm going to send you an application to Howard, and I want it back in my office in two days."

When I received that promised application in the mail, I was excited but thoroughly unprepared to fill it out. It was something I never expected to do. A bit overwhelmed, I visited Mrs. Harris for some guidance. She was so excited! She waved that application around in the air, saying, "Yes, yes! Now we have a chance!" I didn't have access to a typewriter to properly prepare my submission, so Mrs. Harris typed it up for me. We got everything filled out, and I dropped it back in the mail just like Moses requested. Then, we waited.

Two weeks later, I received a response in the mail. I'd allowed myself to get excited about the prospect of college, but the first paragraph of the letter I received burst my bubble. It read, "We are sorry to inform you that you have not been accepted into Howard University School of Arts and Sciences." I almost crumpled it up and tossed in the garbage right then and there, but I resisted the urge. It's a good thing I did, because the letter continued, "However, upon review of your math scores, you might consider applying to the College of Engineering." Looking back, it's obvious that's where I should have applied in the first place. With my 325 SAT score in English—which basically meant I was only able to spell my name on the test correctly—it's

no wonder a school of humanities rejected me. I took the letter back to Mrs. Harris's office and she jumped at the chance to help me reshape my application for the College of Engineering. I mailed it off, and then we waited. Again.

A few weeks later, I received a thick envelope from Howard University—an envelope that changed the course of my life. I was accepted into their College of Engineering! Not only that, but the school recognized my dire financial circumstances and offered grant-in-aid support for me made up of different scholarships and loans that paid 100 percent of my tuition and all textbook costs. It was the definitive turning point in my life. I was going to college!

I walked into Mrs. Harris's office and put my letter of acceptance in her hand. She had the brightest smile on her face as she read the first few lines. "I knew we could do it!" she cried, and a warm wave of acceptance washed over me. She was beaming with pride, and it was all for me. Mrs. Harris then moved over to her intercom and did something I think she'd been waiting to do all year: announce my college acceptance to the world. Back then, a school official made an announcement over the intercom whenever a student was accepted into college. I had listened to those notices for several years and never once thought it would happen for me. But now, every teacher and student at Mainland High School knew I was going to Howard University.

I was walking on air. The full realization of what I'd achieved, my newfound sense of self-worth, and the respect of my classmates gave me a brief break from the feelings of emptiness that always overshadowed me. That day belonged to me—and to my four HAWKs, who'd so generously shared their hearts and convictions in the quest to see me reach my full potential. When I reflect on that day, I'm nearly overcome with feelings of gratitude and blessings. If it hadn't been for the encouragement of those teachers and my providential encounter with Moses Johnson, I never would have attended college or benefited from the opportunities that came with the completion of my degree. It was only in hindsight that I saw the coincidence in his name. Without the encouragement of Moses and my HAWKs, I never would have reached my own promised land.

— **GRADUATION DAY** —

As graduation drew near, I was proud and excited. These were new emotions for me, but I embraced them and prayed they wouldn't leave anytime soon. A few weeks before the commencement ceremony, the school released its graduation invitations for students to buy. They came in packages of five, ten, fifty, and one hundred. I ordered a package of five (that was all I could afford with my lawn-mowing money) and sent them out. The first three went to my mother in Miami, one went to my sister, Mary, and the last, of course, went to my Aunt Katie.

After twelve long years of hard work, excellent grades, unexpected opportunities, and overcoming all kinds of hardships to get there, graduation day finally arrived. I had to be at the school at 6:00 p.m. to find my place in the alphabetical order of graduates. Mary had promised to drive

me there, but she was sitting on the couch at 5:30, clearly not dressed and ready to go. I said, "Mary, aren't you going to get ready?"

I should have expected the response, but it still took me by surprise. She glanced up and said matter-of-factly, "No, I'm just going to drop you off."

That's when it dawned on me. After all I had done, after all I had overcome, no one in my family was coming to celebrate my graduation with me. No one. Not my mother, not my sister, not my brothers—not even my twin. On what should have been the happiest day of my life, I was overwhelmed by a lifetime of emptiness and abandonment that sent me into a state of utter despair. My mother never cared about, never even noticed, any of my accomplishments all through school. All the report cards, academic awards, sports victories, science fairs, and college acceptances in the world couldn't get her attention.

Looking back on that night is hard for me, even after all these decades. True to her word, Mary dropped me off at the front of the school and drove away. All around me, I saw friends and classmates walking into the auditorium with their families. A million proud parents were smiling, laughing, hugging, wiping away tears of pride and joy, and proudly taking photographs with their students. Not me. I hung my head and walked to my seat alone, hoping no one would notice. The bitter disappointment crushed me, and I wept all through the ceremony. To this day, my high school graduation remains the saddest, most depressing day of my life. I cried for five days straight afterward, locking myself away from everyone as I wallowed in a deep depression. Mary and others occasionally asked what was wrong, but I just brushed them off. How could I explain how badly I felt? How could I make them understand how much I had needed them to be there for me for the past eighteen years and how much it hurt when they weren't? I know now that the emotion I was feeling then was grief. I grieved over the fact that my family had essentially ignored every aspect of my life right up to my high school graduation. They'd never recognized anything I'd ever done, and it finally dawned on me that they never would.

That summer, I struggled to get some semblance of equilibrium back into my life. I knew I had to put my past behind me. There was no time for feelings of rejection or self-pity on the journey I was about to undertake. In a few short months, I would be facing the biggest challenge of my life, not to mention my greatest opportunity. I knew I'd have to be at my best, working with discipline and diligence, to make it through Howard. And I was determined to succeed, regardless of how my family behaved. I was on my own, and I hadn't come all that way to fail.

**I was determined to succeed, regardless of how my family behaved. I was on my own, and I hadn't come all that way to fail.**

Most of the people I grew up with let these or similar experiences stop them. They would whine, "Woe is me!"

and stay in the same terrible circumstances for their entire lives. I saw this response all around me in the Black Box and especially in my own family. But I learned early on that you have to aspire to greatness or everything will just bring you down. Life will always throw obstacles in your path, but it's up to you whether those things will be hurdles ... or stepping-stones.

# THREE

## A College Degree on $125 a Year

*"I learned that if you want to make it bad enough, no matter how bad it is, you can make it."*

~ GALE SAYERS ~

After graduating from Mainland in 1969, I had a few months to get ready for college. My main concern was money. I was so grateful to have financial assistance through the school, but it didn't cover things like moving expenses, food, clothes, or other necessities. I knew I had to spend that whole summer working and saving, so I got the best job I could find: working in an auto dealership. I detailed and washed cars so they'd look their best for prospective customers. My car dealer experiences hadn't been that great up to this point, though. I never forgot being chased out of the showroom of Lloyd Cadillac and Buick every week as a boy when all I wanted was a sip of water, and I certainly never forgot the indignity of having to drink from the dirty hose behind the dealership. Sadly, things hadn't changed much in the years since then.

Even though I was a dealership employee now, I still

wasn't allowed in the showroom where customers might see me. I had to remain out back, out of public view. There was so much discrimination back then, I wasn't even allowed to enter the main office and hand the sales manager the keys to the cars. Once I cleaned the vehicles, the white "runners" came by to pick up the keys, and then *they* were the ones who placed them in the hands of the sales manager. The rest of the staff, including my boss, never really saw me as an employee; they treated me like temporary labor that needed to stay out of sight from the "civilized" clientele. It was not an uplifting experience, to say the least.

With what I earned at the dealership that summer, though, I was finally able to buy some new clothes, two steel trunks from the Army-Navy Store, and a one-way plane ticket to Washington, D.C., home of Howard University . . . and my future.

All my worldly possessions fit into those two steel trunks, and, to save money, I had them shipped by Greyhound instead of taking them on the plane. When I boarded my flight, all I had were the clothes on my back, two claim tickets for my luggage, and $125 cash. I had something else going for me, though. I carried with me the knowledge of how to live with hunger. I guess you'd call that a valuable life skill, because that $125 was my *entire* food budget for the next nine months of school. Finally, it was time to go to college.

## — NO COWARDS AT HOWARD —

he moment I stepped out of the D.C. airport, a terrible sense of being overwhelmed washed all over me. I'd just gotten off my first ever airplane ride, and now I was smack-dab in the heart of a huge city with no idea how to get from one place to another. I tried to focus on the immediate tasks: I knew I had to pick up my trunks at the Greyhound station, and then I had to get to my dormitory on Howard's campus. After a lot of thought, I decided the only way to get it all done was to use some of my precious $125 on a taxi. The driver got me to the bus station and waited while I picked up my luggage, and then we were off to the university.

### Trading One Box for Another

I spent that car ride looking out the window, taking in the changing landscape of our nation's capital as we made our way from the airport, to the bus station, and then onto Howard's campus. The neighborhoods out the window had gone from good to bad to worse. That's where we stopped. Howard, though a great school, was located in a terrible part of town. The university was like a box within a box: the smaller box was the Howard campus, which seemed to be placed right in the middle of a miles-wide box of the surrounding city slums. The rough areas of Daytona's Black Box paled in comparison to what I

saw outside the gates of the
university. I was so shaken by the sight that I actually
didn't leave the school grounds for three months—too
scared to enter "the hood."

Fortunately, I was assigned to Drew Hall, where
some upperclassmen befriended me and taught me how to
navigate my way off campus and avoid the dangerous and
unpredictable parts of town. One student, Billie Andrews,
was critical in helping me adjust to my new life at Howard.
Billie and I had been friends and neighbors in the Black Box,
and he was now a Howard sophomore. He taught me how
to beat the class registration lines, showed me good places
to meet coeds (like the wall near the girls' dormitories), and
even how to spot the "fly guys," the cool guys in the local
neighborhoods who always had the inside track on what was
going on, who was who, what was for sale, and how to find
whatever anyone needed.

Billie also gave me some insight into the composition of
the student body. While Mainland High School had been
overwhelmingly white, Howard University was just the
opposite; the vast majority of students were black. That gave
me hope that I wouldn't have to deal with racism and prejudice
at Howard the way I had to during my years at Mainland.

I was also fortunate to have been assigned to the Drew
Hall dorm because of the many bright, promising classmates
who lived there. In fact, so many influential, successful

black Americans came out of Drew Hall over the years that a book was written about them. *The Brotherhood of Drew Hall* was written by Drew Hall alumnus Jeff Burns, Jr., who later became the associate publisher of *Ebony* magazine. It showcased people like Edward T. Welburn, who went on to become the vice president and chief designer of global design at General Motors, meaning he impacted the design of every car GM produced. I was honored to have my own chapter in the book myself.

Encouraged by what Billie taught me and by the excitement of the other students in my dorm, I felt much better equipped to start my classes when they began two weeks after my arrival.

### Starting an Uphill Climb

Howard's legacy and reputation were intimidating. I'd always been one of the brightest students in my school, but now I was sitting side by side with other men and women who seemed just as smart—or smarter—than I was. Right before classes started, the School of Engineering held a mandatory orientation session for all incoming freshmen. I sat in that huge auditorium with two hundred other freshmen engineering students as the administrators told us exactly what to expect over the next few years.

We were reminded that Howard University was ranked in the top third of national universities. Because of its excellent academic reputation and high proportion of black students, it was known as the Harvard University of the black community. The speaker ran through a daunting list of successful graduates, including Pulitzer Prize-winning author Toni Morrison and associate justice of the Supreme Court Thurgood Marshall.

Then he said, "Look to your left, to your right, and then down at yourself. Two of the three of you will not graduate. Only 33 percent of this freshman class will receive diplomas from the School of Engineering. The other two-thirds of you will either fail or drop out."

> **Look to your left, to your right, and then down at yourself. Two of the three of you will not graduate.**

That stat made my heart sink. I was there to *win*; I was determined not to wash out of the engineering program and fall back to my old life in the Black Box. Whatever it took, I knew I was not going to be one of the sixty-seven percent who couldn't make it. I've often wondered in the years since then how much more anxious I would have been if I had known the speaker was being overly optimistic. As it turned out, of the two hundred freshmen in the auditorium that day, only thirty-four of us (a meager 17 percent) would go on to complete the engineering degree. In any case, by the end of that first day, it was completely clear that I was facing the toughest academic challenge of my life. I thought of my HAWKs and their belief in me, and I was inspired. They had been my guardian angels in high school; I could only hope they were watching over me now.

## — PUNCHING IN ... AND PUNCHING OUT —

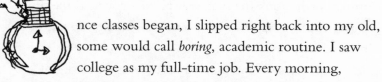

nce classes began, I slipped right back into my old, some would call *boring*, academic routine. I saw college as my full-time job. Every morning, I would wake up and *punch in* like I was punching a time clock. I went to class during the day, and then I returned to my dorm to study until late into the evening. I carried eighteen credit hours of classes that term, and I studied eight hours a day every single day. Between sitting in class and sitting in the dorm studying, I was in total school mode from 7:30 a.m. when I woke up until 1:00 a.m. when I finally closed my books for the night. It was relentless, and there were times I was grateful for my natural social introversion. While my new friends were going out every night and partying, I was more comfortable staying home. That kept me out of a lot of the trouble they got into, trouble that eventually led many of them to *punch out*—the term we used to refer to fellow classmates who burned out, dropped out, or failed out of school.

The first-year engineering courses were rigorous and part of a lock-step sequence that left little room for success unless students were seriously committed to study. In the first year, we all took Chemistry 1, Physics 1, and Calculus, along with the other required courses. The course of study in the engineering school was unforgiving; if a student didn't pass Chemistry 1 in the first semester, he was ineligible to take Chemistry 2 in the spring. That immediately put him one year behind his classmates, an instant setback that sent many heartbroken students home early. I remember one of my dormmates who took the first-year physics course three times. He never could wrap his head around it. Needless to say, he didn't graduate.

It became clear to me that many students failed out of the engineering program for one of two main reasons: they were either unprepared for or incapable of doing the hard work the program demanded of us, or they couldn't resist the temptations associated with college life and the newfound freedoms of young adulthood.

Preparation wasn't an issue for me. It quickly became apparent just how well my HAWKs and their advanced classes had prepared me for rigorous university studies. In my first two years at Howard, in fact, much of the material that was new to my classmates was a simple review of what I'd already learned. I was perfectly comfortable with the material and able to engage my teachers in informed discussions about it, but many of the students around me struggled to get their heads around it for the first time.

The other cause of student attrition was even more disappointing. While some students couldn't get a handle on their coursework, others couldn't get a handle on their partying. This is all too common on college campuses, and Howard was no exception. Drugs, alcohol, casual sex, and nonstop parties wrecked many classmates' academic aspirations. Unhealthy or "too much, too fast" relationships knocked out several others. Sometimes, a student struggled with one or two of these things; other times, someone would fall victim to all of them at once. I remember one guy in Drew Hall who partied that entire first year. He always had girls going in and out of his room, and we always saw a towel wrapped around his dorm-room doorknob—a signal letting us know he had a girl in there. That guy must have had a thousand dates that year. The one date he never got, though, was a *graduation* date. He punched out in his second year.

Getting used to life on my own at Howard took some time, but all my hard work and my monastic study schedule paid off at the end of my first term. I earned As in calculus, physics, and chemistry, but I got a D in drafting. I was disappointed because it brought down my grade point average, but I realized it wouldn't be a real problem in my career. Once I was a working engineer, other people would do the drafting for me.

Ever since the eighth grade, I'd wanted to become an engineer. Now, with one semester of college behind me, I realized my longtime goal was within reach.

## — SECOND SEMESTER CHANGES —

With my first term behind me, I took stock of where I was and what changes I'd need to make to ensure my ongoing success at Howard. Two things stood out to me: First, I realized I needed to do more than hide in my room studying all the time. I knew employers looked at more than just a graduate's grades; they looked at his entire college life. If I wanted to really stand out to future employers, I needed to add some extracurricular activities to my résumé. Second, I needed to reevaluate my food budget. The $125 I brought to school with me—which I had beefed up to $300 after saving money on textbooks by buying used copies—was getting stretched far too thin. I was hungry *all the time,* just like I'd been back in the Black Box growing up. It was time to try and change that.

### Starve or Swim

During my first term, I literally survived on one hot dog a day at lunchtime, which I bought for fifty cents from a campus vending machine. When I got really hungry, I'd go across the street from campus and eat at the neighborhood greasy spoon. That was always an experience. The waitress was gruff and growly, and she always demanded payment up front before she'd serve me. She was exactly like the "Soup Nazi" from Seinfeld. It was clear that she'd been stiffed one too many times by locals who would eat and run. That wasn't a huge problem for me, though, because I could rarely afford to go over there.

**The waitress was gruff and growly, and she always demanded payment up front before she'd serve me.**

Trying to find a solution to both of these problems, and with the school's swimming season right around the corner, I tried out for the swim team as a walk-on diver. This turned out to be a great decision. I made the team, which opened up a new world of friends to me and, in turn, gave me access to the school cafeteria. Athletes with scholarships got to eat three meals a day at the cafeteria for free. I couldn't even imagine such a golden ticket. Even though I was on the team that semester, though, I didn't have an athletic scholarship and couldn't *officially* eat at the cafeteria. Fortunately, a friend and teammate named Nate Harris often snuck me into the cafeteria to eat with him, and I was able to eat as much as I wanted in there. I even took a lot of food with me when I left (which students weren't supposed to do) to eat later. This new windfall of food supplemented my meager meal budget and enabled me to finish the year without starving to death. And, as it turned out, Nate's girlfriend, Cynthia, grew up a couple of streets over from me in the Black Box. Her mother was even my first-grade teacher! Small world—and one of many examples of providence in my life story.

## Young Love

By the beginning of my second semester, I was really starting to feel at home in my new world. My courses were challenging but manageable, thanks to the advanced classes and great teachers I had in high school. I was making new friends on the swim team and, because of them, I no longer had to survive on one hot dog a day. Life was good, and it was about to get better.

Growing up in the Black Box, I'd always tried to keep

my head down, stay out of trouble, and put all my time and energy into my studies. That, plus my natural introversion, left no room for girls in my life. To be blunt, I'd never even had a date. But then I met Mattie, a beautiful coed from New York. She and I instantly clicked, and Mattie became my first date and my first girlfriend at the same time. We had so much in common, not the least of which was our commitment to education. We shared a passion to graduate, and we both had the academic talent, focus, and discipline to get there. We both avoided parties and probably only went to one or two together during the three years we dated. Most of our dates were instead centered around studying, which we did for hours on end. Truthfully, I'd never experienced such intense romantic feelings for a woman until I met Mattie, but my strong physical attraction was tempered by her anxiety about intimacy and, more specifically, her fear of becoming pregnant. In those days, birth control pills and other contraceptives were hard to come by, and Mattie knew too many girls who'd dropped out of school because of a pregnancy. She had no intention of becoming one of them, and I couldn't blame her. So, while we did kiss and have *some* physical connection, let's just say I never really needed to tie a towel to my doorknob.

Mattie was an integral part of my success at Howard. From the day we met, I never went out with another girl during all my years there. There was no need; I knew I'd never find a better fit for me during that season of my life. She was my friend, study partner, encourager, and confidant. Mattie was also the first person I confided in about my childhood, and she held my secrets tenderly. When she graduated three years later, Mattie moved back home to New York while I moved elsewhere to start my career. We quickly lost touch in those days before email or social networking, but I have often thought fondly about her and the incredible impact she's made on countless children as a teacher. Even though we went our separate ways, I'll always appreciate our time together and the significant impact she had on my academic career.

## A Fraternity with Opportunity

As I settled into that second semester of my freshman year, I had a few pockets of time left between study dates with Mattie and swim practice. Still looking to round out my college experience, I added two new things to my life that term. First, I joined the Reserve Officer Training Cadet (ROTC) drill team. It was a commitment that required one hour of practice every day, Monday through Friday, over the lunch hour. Because I often didn't eat lunch, it wasn't much of a strain on my schedule. The practice involved throwing rifles over our heads and marching in unison. We tossed those rifles with such proficiency that we managed to finish third in the national competition held in Phoenix, Arizona. To get there, the Air Force provided a cargo plane for our whole team.

We had to sit crammed against the outer carriage wall of the aircraft, because there were no seats. Making things worse, the fuselage of the aircraft was curved, making sitting for any length of time less than comfortable. That flight lasted twelve hours, but, in the end, it was a completely unique experience that was well worth it.

The second new commitment I made that semester was joining a fraternity. I know, after reading so much about my introversion and resistance to the college party lifestyle, it may sound strange to know I was a member of a fraternity. But this was a much different group of men than the others on campus. My friend Billie Andrews was a member of Alpha Phi Omega, a national service fraternity, and he encouraged me to join. I knew most male students at Howard pledged themselves to fraternities in the second semester of their first year. Joining was free and, in the end, Billie convinced me.

What attracted me to Alpha Phi Omega was their commitment to service. While other national fraternities focused on partying, Alpha Phi Omega emphasized helping others in the community, usually the less fortunate and underprivileged of society. To become a full-fledged member of the fraternity, pledges had to go through the rite of passage known as hazing before they were fully initiated as brothers. Hazing has been known to get out of control and has since been banned on most college campuses, but my own experience wasn't that bad. It lasted about two months, during which I had to learn about the history of

the fraternity, get to know the members, and carry out all
sorts of mundane member requests like fetching meals and
doing laundry. Only the pledges who were able to keep their
eyes on the prize and carry out those tasks successfully were
ultimately inducted into the fraternity as bona fide members.
But first, we had to get through the induction ceremony,
which was no easy feat.

It came by surprise, because they didn't tell us when it
would happen, but once it started, it went on for the entire
night. To begin with, each pledge had to be drunk, and
whisky was the instrument of choice. It shouldn't be a surprise
to learn this was the first time I was ever drunk. Then, each
pledge was *tarred and feathered*: honey was poured all over our
bodies, followed by Rice Krispies and feathers. I remember
the members laughing at us as they performed this ritual.
I also remember throwing up throughout the ordeal. Just
before dawn, all us pledges were blindfolded and driven
through Washington, D.C., drunk and covered in goo. It was
completely disorienting. When the cars finally
stopped, they pulled us out and lined us all
up. Finally, after an incredibly long night,
they yelled, "Take off your blindfolds!
Now!" We obeyed and looked up, and
right in front of us was the magnificent
Lincoln Monument, all lit up in the pre-
dawn darkness. I'll never forget
that sight—and yes, the true
feeling of camaraderie—while

we were congratulated on becoming full-fledged members of Alpha Phi Omega service fraternity.

That kind of wild hazing ritual might give the impression that Alpha Phi Omega was just another reckless, frivolous, superficial, party-driven social fraternity. Nothing could be further from the truth. Sure, we had fun together and engaged in some sophomoric silliness, but we remained focused on our goal: to serve the less fortunate people all around us. Every weekend, we undertook some service project that would help the needy or clean up neglected areas of the city. In all, the hours we spent *playing* together were far outweighed by the hours we spent *serving* together.

It was through Alpha Phi Omega that I was first introduced to the idea of helping others in need and the practice of charitable giving. Those experiences left a lasting impression on me and helped me discover my true calling: to help those in poverty become productive, self-supporting members of society. You might say this was when my "charity gene" was activated for the first time.

Some have asked me why I never spent any time serving or giving before then, and my response is pretty simple: it's hard to give to the least of these when you technically *are* one of the least of these. Before Alpha Phi Omega, I had neither the means nor the motivation to give back. That changed later in life, of course, as my financial success allowed me to offer my time and treasures to those who needed it. Until then, I busied myself with helping others through Alpha Phi Omega's charitable activities. It was easy to feel compassion

for those people and to know how important our help was.
Just one year earlier, I was struggling to survive in the Black
Box and was thrilled whenever a service organization came
through the area to help out. In fact,
I realized just how far my life had
come when I was assigned the task of
tidying up a vacant lot that was full of
abandoned garbage cans. Now I was
cleaning them up instead of eating
out of them.

> **Just one year earlier, I was struggling to survive in the Black Box and was thrilled whenever a service organization came through the area to help out.**

Alpha Phi Omega gave me the
opportunity to take stock of my life,
acknowledge how far I'd come, and
reflect on all the good things that
had come my way. I'd always thought
engineering was my passion, but I soon realized helping others
was truly what made my heart sing. Engineering, it turned out,
was simply the means to get me there. It was then, in the spring
of 1970, that I made a pledge to dedicate the rest of my life to
helping those in need.

### Swimming across the Finish Line

That whole first year flew by in a blur. Between studying,
classes, spending time with Mattie, practicing with the
drill team, serving with Alpha Phi Omega, and, of course,
swimming, I stayed busy all day every day. Taking stock of
the year as a whole, I realized that joining the swim team had

been an especially good decision, and I was so glad I had taken
a chance and tried out for a rare walk-on spot. I was also proud
of my performance on the team, and all the guys had become
good friends. My biggest swim victory, however, came in our
final team meeting for the year. After discussing what we had
accomplished and how we could improve for next year's season,
the coach wished us all a good summer. Then, as we got up to
leave, he said, "Wait! I almost forgot. This past season, you all
worked hard, but one person in particular went the extra mile
and really impressed me." He pointed to me and said, "I'm so
proud of you, Tony, and of what you've accomplished." Then
he said something that changed my life: "And I'm excited to
award you a *full scholarship* for next year!"

I couldn't believe it. That scholarship meant the world to me.
It obviously meant that I didn't have to worry about paying any
tuition or taking any school loans for the next year, but the thing
I was most excited about was the cafeteria access. As an athlete
with a scholarship, I could walk into that beautiful cafeteria three
times a day—every day—and eat whatever I wanted. For the
first time in my life, I didn't have to worry about how, when,
and where to find a scrap of food. More importantly, as long
as I stayed on the swim team throughout the rest of my college
career and got a job when I was finished, I knew my lifelong
struggle with hunger was finally over. I had gone from dumpster
diving to springboard diving, and there would be no more
rotten fruit, moldy cake, or tapeworms in my future. It was an
incredible way to head into my sophomore year!

## — SAVING MONEY WHILE SAVING LIVES —

Just like that, my first year of college was over, and I had to figure out how to spend my summer. Obviously, that meant finding work. Even with my scholarship, I knew I'd need money to make it through my sophomore year, and my savings were completely depleted. I didn't think I'd find any good work in Daytona Beach, so I headed down to Miami. With my experience on the swim team, it was easy to find work as a lifeguard at a community swimming pool. I didn't want to live with my mother, who'd moved to Miami years earlier, so I rented a no-frills room from a strict lady who needed the extra income. I spent my nights there and my days at the pool, guarding the swimmers in thirty-minute shifts, rotating off and on with another lifeguard. The law required us to take those thirty-minute shift intervals; sitting in the hot sun and watching a pool full of people for signs of distress is not as easy as it looks.

When people hear I used to work as a lifeguard, they often ask if I've ever saved someone from drowning. Yes, I have. The truth is, I saved someone at least once a day every day that I worked. The kids were the worst. They often thought they could swim, even if they'd never had lessons. I'd see them jump into the deep end of the pool and end up in a world of trouble. At least the older swimmers knew better than that.

I have to admit, though, that the kids weren't the only ones acting foolishly at the pool that summer. I made my own share of mistakes, and one of them almost cost me my life. While practicing my diving one day, I attempted a two-and-a-half rotation summersault. I didn't make it. Instead, I hit the back of my head on the diving board and crashed into the water, filling the pool with blood. It took eighteen stitches to patch up the nasty gash in my head, but I was lucky. The doctor told me if I'd rotated just a quarter of an inch farther before hitting the board, I would have broken my neck.

Aside from that one potentially life-changing accident, it was a busy, fruitful summer. I saved a lot of swimmers from drowning, worked on my diving skills, and managed to save $400 for my return to school. That may not seem like much now, but, for a kid from the Black Box in the early 1970s, it felt like a fortune. One year earlier, I was heading to Howard for the first time nervous, alone, and with only $125 in my pocket. Now, it was time to see what I could do with a steady girlfriend, fraternity brothers, good friends, strong grades, a full scholarship, and $400. I was ready for year two!

## — MY INTRODUCTION TO GENERAL MOTORS —

s my sophomore year started, I felt much more secure and stable than I did the previous year. I had survived the crucible of crises that every college freshman has to go through, and I'd come out stronger for it. Now, it was time to get back to work. I slipped right back into my old, familiar groove with my studies, and I continued to enjoy competing with the swim team, practicing with the drill team, and serving with my fraternity. Midway through the year, though, a new opportunity arose—one that would define my college years and entire career.

### Internship and Opportunities

Every engineering student had to participate in an extended internship as part of the degree requirements. We had to find our own internship, and it would last from late spring of the second year through the end of that summer. Then we'd resume classes in the fall. All of us wracked our brains trying to find the best internship opportunities across the country. The buzz around campus was that General Motors (GM) offered the best pay to their interns. There was a daunting downside, though: GM had a difficult application process and fierce competition. I had never let those things stop me in the past, however, and I had no intention of doing so now. So, I filled out the application, dropped it in the mail, and hoped for the best. I was thrilled a few weeks later when I got my acceptance letter. I was going to intern at GM!

**There was a daunting downside, though: GM had a difficult application process and fierce competition.**

At the end of spring semester, I took a Greyhound bus to Detroit and checked into the Holiday Inn right across the street from the General Motors building. The company paid the bill for temporary hotel accommodation, but that meant we all had

to share a room with another intern to keep the costs down.
I met my roommate, Steve, the day we arrived, and we chatted
about how excited we were to get the chance to work at GM's
World Headquarters of Engineering (WHE). Neither of us had
a car, but we didn't think that'd be a problem since our plan
was to find a cheap place to live close by and simply walk across
the street to work every day. Unfortunately, things didn't quite
work out as we planned. We were surprised to learn that the
WHE was a separate complex located in Warren, Michigan,
fifteen miles away from the main GM office. With just a week
to go before we had to report for work, Steve and I had to solve
our housing and transportation problems—and *fast*.

Lucky for us, one of our classmates, a guy named Leroy,
was also interning at GM that summer. His aunt lived in an
apartment in a rough neighborhood in downtown Detroit, and
she offered to take us in as tenants. We gratefully accepted, but
her home was crowded and a bit dingy. It reminded me a lot
of living back in the Black Box and was certainly a step down
from living in the dorms at Howard, but we were happy to
have a place to sleep. We knew we'd be spending most of our
time at work, anyway.

That just left the transportation problem. Steve and I
worked together on this one. We scoured the newspaper for
a few days until the perfect car popped up
in the classifieds. It was a pale blue 1957
Plymouth with white stripes, and the
owner only wanted $150 for it. Steve
and I checked it out and thought it

was a pretty good deal, so we went in together to buy it. It was my first car—a far cry from the shiny red Mustang convertible Mrs. Aumiller let me drive back in high school, but it was *mine.* Well, mine and Steve's, I guess.

## Reporting for Work

I reported for work at General Motors for the first time on June 19, 1971. Our first stop was the Human Resources office, where we received two cards: one blue and one yellow. Every person who worked at GM received these cards. The blue one was for the employee's physical, given to the onsite doctor who determined if you were fit for work. Once you had his signature, you were cleared to start your job. The yellow card was infamous; it's what GM used to get you to sign your life away. By signing this card, each employee agreed that anything he or she invented while working at the company belonged to General Motors, *not* the employee. That meant if I invented something that made GM billions of dollars, they still wouldn't owe me a dime for the idea. But GM was not without mercy; for each patent an engineer secured, he or she received a plaque with a dollar bill embossed in the center. It was really meant to be a symbolic award in recognition of the engineer's accomplishment, but it still makes me laugh that engineers got one dollar for each of their groundbreaking ideas.

That first day started full of promise and excitement, but it turned sour pretty quickly when I learned Steve failed his physical. It was apparently something serious, but he hadn't told me the details of his health during the time we'd spent together the previous week. We were ready to start this adventure together—we got a car and a place to stay—and then the doctor told him he had to go home. I couldn't imagine his disappointment. The last time I saw him, he was walking out the door, suitcase in hand, headed for home. He didn't return to school. In fact, I never saw him again.

Two weeks after Steve left, the Plymouth blew its engine. Fortunately, my other roommate Leroy had connections and found someone willing to drive both of us to and from work. Still, I couldn't shake the feeling that Steve's health crisis and the demise of the Plymouth were bad omens. I tried to shake off the gloom and worry by diving into my work. After all, I'd dreamt of working as an engineer my entire life, and here I was working at General Motors' World Headquarters of Engineering. I was exactly where I'd always hoped to be, and I planned on making the most of this opportunity.

Fitting in at GM, though, felt like starting at Mainland High School all over again. It took ten minutes to navigate the length of the huge building, among an overwhelming landscape of white faces. I was a minority among more than three thousand white engineers, but, truthfully, it didn't really bother me anymore. It was just a motivating reminder of how rare it was for a black man to make it as an engineer.

That initial GM internship went remarkably well. I was busy testing automobile parts that had been put through the paces at proving grounds with extreme climates, like Arizona and Alaska. As much as I enjoyed my work, returning to my temporary home with Leroy was great too. Plus, there was an unexpected bonus: the modest monthly room and board I paid Leroy's aunt included three meals a day, and she was an incredible cook. I remember watching her working in the kitchen and the smell of the incredible soul food she served. She even packed lunches for me to take to work, and I swear she made the greatest sandwiches in the world. Lettuce, tomato, ham, and cheese! I'd never had a sandwich like it. Sometimes she packed a leftover chicken sandwich with a few cranberries hidden inside for a tangy surprise. I can taste them even now. After getting used to a year of three cafeteria meals a day with my swimming scholarship, I was so grateful to not have to worry about food for the summer. It made me truly start to believe that my days of going hungry were gone for good.

By the time that internship ended, I was far from a full-fledged engineer, but I'd learned a lot and gained a good understanding of what engineers did and how they did it. Now, it was time to get back to school and focus on graduating and getting back to engineering as quickly as possible.

## — RACING TO THE FINISH LINE —

got back to Howard that fall and entered my junior year at full stride. My internship had fired up my desire to become an engineer to an even higher level, and I tore into my studies with renewed vigor. I decided to quit the drill team to concentrate more on my coursework, but I still found the time for my fraternity's service projects. I was taking eighteen credit hours of the most difficult courses in the engineering school (a full load was twelve to fifteen hours) and doing well. Like a snowball gaining size and momentum as it rolls down a hillside, I was making progress toward my degree faster and more efficiently than I ever imagined. Even so, I decided it was time to push the envelope and see what I was *really* capable of.

Howard University's School of Engineering was a five-year degree program, but I became obsessed with finishing my degree a full semester early. I mapped out a plan and started attacking it as soon as my junior year classes began. The first step was taking an extra course that fall. When I saw I could handle the extra coursework without sacrificing my grades, I took the next step, which was taking additional engineering courses at the Detroit Institute of Technology when I returned to General Motors for my required fifteen-month internship at the end of junior year. The extra coursework definitely turned up the pressure, but I found I was able to manage everything without dropping any balls. That gave me the confidence I needed to take the final (and most ambitious) step: enroll in twenty-four credit hours of courses for the final semester my senior year. I honestly wasn't convinced I could pull that off. This basically meant completing two semesters worth of courses in one term. I don't know if anyone had ever tried that before or has tried it since; in fact, most engineering schools these days won't even allow students to try it. I got permission and, as if that wasn't enough, got extra work teaching a course in computer science for social sciences students. The funny thing was, I was *teaching* "Computers in Society" while I was *taking* the engineering version of the class myself!

> **The funny thing was, I was *teaching* "Computers in Society" while I was *taking* the engineering version of the class myself.**

It's reasonable to wonder why I worked so hard to graduate in December rather than waiting five months to graduate with the rest of my class the following May. Despite what some of my friends joked at the time, I certainly was not a masochist. I had some good reasons—reasons that set me up for a great start to my career. First, by graduating a semester early, I knew I'd have a five-month head start on the job search, beating my classmates to the punch. Second and more importantly, I already had a great job offer from GM at their World Headquarters of Engineering, where I'd interned the past two years. There was a catch, though: the offer was only good to the end of the calendar year. There was no guarantee it would be there if I waited until graduation in May. In my mind, then, the choice was clear. I could work my tail off to graduate in December with a guaranteed job in hand, or I could finish my degree in May and gamble on finding a job at the same time as my classmates.

For a guy who'd dreamed of becoming an engineer his entire life and who'd overcome incredible obstacles to get there, the choice was clear. I decided to go for it, and I never looked back. In retrospect, graduating early was probably the hardest thing I've ever done in my life. I spent that entire semester running from one class to the next, studying, and teaching. There were no breaks, no slowing down, and no rest; it was just a relentless race toward the end. Every day, though, the finish line got a little closer and a little more within reach. That was all I needed.

Then, suddenly, it was over. I took my final exam on Friday, December 14, 1973. The moment I handed the instructor my papers, a huge wave of emotion washed over me. There I was in the exam hall, crying my eyes out. I thought, *Tony, you did it! You're an electrical engineer, something you've wanted to be since you were twelve years old!* I was done with college and had a great engineering job waiting for me. It was a dream come true, and I wanted to celebrate. But how? I remembered there was a movie everyone had been raving about. I had been so covered up with schoolwork my entire college career that I hadn't been to a movie theater since I'd arrived at Howard. So, I went to the local movie house and watched *The Godfather.* I soaked in that movie while floating on a cloud, knowing I had accomplished my objective. The elation and relief I felt that afternoon was greater than I could ever describe. It was truly the high point of my life up to that point.

The next morning, I packed my car and began the drive back to Detroit, toward my future. I finished college on a Friday and by Monday morning I was reporting to work at General Motors. In a single weekend, I had gone from being a student to being an engineer. And boy, was I ready. I was ready to work!

# FOUR

# Passion, Patents, and Promotions

"Success is how high you bounce
when you hit bottom."
~ GENERAL GEORGE PATTON ~

ecember 17, 1973, was the start of a whole new life for me. It had been a long, hard road, but I had made it. I was no longer a struggling student. I wasn't a poor kid living in squalor. I wasn't a scared and lonely child desperately seeking the approval of his absent and abusive mother. Those things were all still a *part* of me, of course—they always will be—but they weren't who I *was* anymore. Starting this day, I was an engineer. A professional, full-time engineer beginning a promising career with one of the world's most successful automotive companies. Everything about my life changed forever on that day as I walked into GM as a full-time employee.

## — BODY BY FISHER, PATENTS BY MARCH —

he iconic Body by Fisher symbol is well-known to anyone who owned a GM vehicle well into the 1990s. The Body by Fisher division of GM was responsible for every component of the company's automobiles from the windshield to the tailpipe across all brands and models, including Pontiac, Buick, Cadillac, Oldsmobile, GMC, and Chevrolet. This is where I landed in my first job as an electrical engineer. Right from the start of my career, I had the opportunity to make a real, hands-on, noticeable difference to most of the cars I saw out on the street. It was a dream come true, and an opportunity I planned on making the most of—even when others thought I'd fail.

### New Challenges Every Day

My first assignment was digitizing the clay models of GM's various cars. Believe it or not, every GM car back then started out as a full-sized clay model that was reworked, revamped, tweaked, and calibrated until top management was satisfied with it. Only then was the vehicle put into production. These days, of course, we can do all that design work on a computer, but back in the 1970s, we literally molded cars out of clay.

It was an exciting time for someone with my qualifications. I was lucky to be the only electrical engineer in my department at the precise time my specialization was becoming an integral part of how cars were being manufactured. My goal was to turn mechanically functioning parts of the car into systems that worked electronically. And I was busy! Every two or three months, from my first day of work until I left GM many years later, I always had some new, innovative project to work on. I was promoted to the electromechanical department within six months and my career took off from there. Day in and day out, I was creating, testing, and implementing new devices that would improve GM's automotive product with cutting-edge technology.

Just like I'd done all through school, I slipped into a routine of working morning, noon, and night. Sometimes, it felt like I was there all day, every day. In time, other people started to notice. I was working late one evening, hours after everyone else in my department had gone home. Body by Fisher employed three thousand engineers, and I figured the other 2,999 were already at home, preparing for bed. But I was wrong. There was one other engineer still in the building, but he wasn't *just* an engineer. He was Ed Mertz, our chief engineer and, in our world, the boss of bosses.

Mr. Mertz was on his way to the parking lot, which took him directly past my post. I was in my typical position, sprawled across my drafting table, repositioning a solenoid switch, when he came up behind me. "Every time I walk by, you're here working," he said. He asked what I was doing, and I gave him a quick breakdown of my little project: the first programmable memory seat option to be offered in a General Motors vehicle. Mr. Mertz nodded his approval and told me how impressed he was by my work ethic and how proud he was of my contributions to the company. To this day, that was one of the most memorable compliments I ever received.

### The Holy Grail of Engineering

Of course, the ultimate praise was saved for those engineers who were granted patents, the holy grail of our profession. The vast majority of engineers at GM never secured a patent in their entire careers; I was fortunate enough to get three. The first involved miniaturizing a switch that operated a car's power trunk. The second simplified the system that controlled a six-way seat switch. My third patent was for the project Ed Mertz stumbled upon, the memory seat option (an electronic module that allowed the driver to program a customized seat position).

> **I got a grand total of $3—a single dollar bill for each of my patents.**

In all, it's hard to say how much money GM made or saved because of my three patents, but it's at least in the tens of millions. My second patent was especially valuable to GM, as they implemented my ideas across the entire General Motors' assembly line. They saved $33 million over a three-year period from this one patent alone. And how much did I receive in bonuses in return for saving the company so much money? I got a grand total of $3—a single dollar bill for each of my patents. That was the price of signing the little yellow employment card, remember?

I wasn't that concerned with the money, though. The real

value of the patents to me was the respect that came along
with it. That was priceless to me. Back then, prejudice was
still alive and well in the workplace, and employees routinely
made racist and sexist comments that would surely get them
fired today. Early in my career, before I won my first patent,
some of my white peers would look down on me and treat
me like an errand boy. They'd say, "Hey, boy. Go get me
some coffee," or they'd try to get me to do other non-
engineering tasks they didn't want to do for themselves. It
was annoying and insulting, but it was just something I had to
live with. That's what made my first patent such a remarkable
achievement for me.

I'll always remember the day I got that first patent. Soon
after it was finalized by the U.S. Patent Office, my boss
walked up to me with something behind his back. Then, in
front of all the other engineers, he called out my name and
handed me a personalized plaque with a $1 bill embossed on it,
congratulating me on receiving my first patent. I looked down
at the plaque in my hands and had the strangest thought: *Wow,
black engineers can get patents too!* It's something I knew *could*
happen, but now I knew it *does* happen—because I had done it.
From that day on, the other engineers looked at me differently.
They finally saw me as a colleague, as a well-trained engineer
who was quickly becoming an expert
in his field. Prejudice didn't dry up
overnight, but the atmosphere
of racism receded a little more
every year. And, of course, the

fact that I was beating my white colleagues in the patent race sped up the process a little bit for me.

## — LEARNING TO LOVE —

I was focused intently on my career that first year on the job, but work wasn't the *only* thing on my mind in 1974. I also had two major personal milestones that year: one I should have expected...and a second I never saw coming.

### Graduation Day

In May, I took a short leave of absence to attend my college graduation. Although I had finished my coursework a semester early the December before, I waited to receive my diploma at the May graduation with the rest of my class. This should have been a moment of triumph—the crowning achievement from my four and a half years of hard work and academic success at a renowned college. But it wasn't. Instead, it was an encore performance of the deep disappointment I felt during and after my high school graduation. Although I had sent out graduation announcements and invitations, no one in my family bothered to attend my commencement. Even worse, nobody even contacted me at all. There were no cards or phone calls, no words of congratulations of any kind. It was as if my mother, brothers, sister, nieces, nephews, cousins, and everyone else I'd known all my life had dropped off the face of the earth. Once again, I had let myself hope *someone* would show up, and, once again, they made me feel foolish for it.

What rationale could there be for a parent to miss her son's college graduation? I don't know what my mother was doing that day; I assume she was doing nothing at all. After a lifetime of neglect, this was the moment I realized once and for all that my family would never—never—recognize any achievement I ever made, no matter what. All the heartbreak and despair from their past rejections came flooding over me. I could feel a familiar, foreboding sense of darkness setting in, of being utterly alone and unloved. All these decades later, I can look back and identify that moment as the beginning of another round of depression. But, at the time, all I knew was that my family had let me down again. I should have been flying high emotionally as I drove back to Detroit with my college degree in hand; instead, it was one of the saddest, most emotionally draining moments of my life.

**No one in my family bothered to attend my commencement. There were no cards or phone calls, no words of congratulations.**

That experience forced me to confront a harsh truth about myself: I suffered from depression. I'd been in and out of bouts of depression throughout my life up to that point, but this was the first time I realized my depression was something I needed to pay careful attention to. I made the hard decision to seek professional help soon afterward and saw my first therapist a few months after my college graduation. Therapy was life-changing for me, and it's something I've maintained ever since. But counseling wasn't the only big change in store for me after graduation. I had a huge surprise waiting for me when I got back to work.

## Loved at Last

I returned to work and kept my head down as I made the long walk to my desk and the backlog of work that surely awaited. I didn't look up until I was just a few feet from my desk. When I did, I had to do a quick double take to make sure I was in the right office because someone was sitting in my chair and working at my desk. It was a woman.

I'd never seen her before, and I certainly couldn't say this out loud, but I was overcome with how beautiful she was. It took a second for me to collect myself enough to ask who she was and why she was sitting behind my desk. She replied, "Oh, hi. Gail Broussard. I'm in the co-op program at GM while I finish my master's degree in electrical engineering. I was assigned to work at your desk until you came back."

For some reason I can't fathom—let's call it nerves and lack of experience with beautiful women—I eked out a horribly sexist comment about female engineers. I'm ashamed to say that now, especially after I'd been forced to overcome so much prejudice myself. Fortunately, Gail didn't write me off completely for my verbal gaffe (although she did tell me how stupid the comment was a few days later).

In fact, aside from that one blunder, she and I hit it off and started spending all our free time together. We had a lot in common, including a passion for education and high career ambitions. She was from New Orleans and was the fifth of thirteen children. Gail spent a lot of time watching her father, who worked as a postman, fix and fine-tune all the neighbors' electronics. Her family encouraged her to pursue an education, and she completed her first undergraduate degree in physics before heading to the University of Detroit for her second undergraduate degree, this one in electrical engineering. That led her into a master's program ... and ultimately to my desk.

Things with Gail went quickly. We first met on May 5, 1974, and were engaged to be married by May 31. It's strange that two highly detailed engineers would move that quickly in a relationship, but neither of us could resist the pull of what was clearly love at first sight. Besides, I think I somehow managed to meet all of the high standards she had set for herself and any potential suitors. I didn't drink, party, or even socialize that much. I had a good job with strong prospects and security, a nice car, and big ambitions. I think I checked off all the items on her list and then some. Most importantly, I understood Gail's drive and motivation, because I approached life the same way. She could be confident that I wasn't going to hold her back.

As for me, within one month, the most beautiful and intelligent woman I'd ever known had fallen in love with me, cooked several delicious meals for me, sewn two shirts and a suit for me, and had reignited my relationship with God. This was a love I'd never experienced, but I was hooked. We set a wedding date for December 21, 1974.

I still had one important job to do before our relationship went too far. Back then, it was a sign of respect for a suitor to go to a woman's father and ask for his permission to marry his daughter. Things had happened so quickly with Gail that I hadn't had a chance to even meet her parents yet, so I set out for New Orleans to win their approval. Gail always joked with her siblings that she was their father's favorite of his thirteen children. She was always the first to rush to the door to greet him when he got home from work, and they had a very special relationship. And now I had to ask this man if I could take his daughter away. No pressure there. Fortunately for us, both of her parents really liked me, and they told their daughter she'd "found a good one."

We were married in New Orleans that December and had an ... understated ... two-night honeymoon at a Holiday Inn down the street from the wedding reception. As soon as we walked through the door of the hotel room, we collapsed into bed exhausted and immediately fell asleep. We slept for fifteen hours straight, waking up together for the first time the next day, ready to start our wonderful new life as husband and wife.

## Learning What Love Means

By that time in life, I'd created a theory based on the relationships I'd experienced thus far. I decided there were only two kinds of people in the world: those who stood by you in the best and worst of times and those who didn't. I call them *crystal balls* and *rubber balls*. To me, rubber balls are your pseudo-friends. They're here today while things are good, but they bounce away as soon as stuff gets real. Crystal balls, on the other hand, stay by your side, helping you see a better future. Think about who'd stand with you and stay by your side if you suddenly became gravely ill for an extended period of time. You'd find out very quickly who your crystal balls are. They'll be the ones driving you to appointments and filling your fridge with soup.

Gail was the one who crystallized—pardon the pun—that theory for me. They say you can't choose your family, and it's true that I didn't choose the people I spent my childhood with. But within one month of meeting her, I chose Gail Broussard to be my family. She was all the family I had and all I needed. She was my crystal ball.

I've made a lot of good decisions in my life, but none of them hold a candle to my decision to marry Gail. The benefits were abundant and immediate. The biggest change for me was the realization that she loved me—she really, truly *loved me*. I'd never had that before. "Home" had always been a place I had to endure, but with Gail, it was a place I felt accepted and adored. The two great hungers of my life had always been food and acceptance, and now my stomach and my heart were both filled to the brim. Gail showed me how to love and how to be loved, as well as how to relax and trust in all the happiness and security that love created. It was all so new to me because love never existed in my family growing up. Once I got a taste for it, I couldn't get enough.

> **Even when I accomplished something small, she'd blow it out of proportion and make me feel like it was the most important thing in the world.**

I didn't know what appreciation felt like until I met my wife. Once we were married, though, our home was overflowing with appreciation. Whenever I won an award or was mentioned in the paper, Gail wrote it up or clipped the article and put it in a scrapbook. She even went back and found all my articles and awards from high school and college and put them in a scrapbook as a surprise. I vividly remember the day she gave it to me and the deep feeling of love I felt. It was something a mother should have done for me. Even when I accomplished something small, she'd blow it out of proportion and make me feel like it was the most important thing in the world. She was the wind beneath my wings, and I was on cloud nine.

## A Gift from Heaven

Because of everything I went through as a child, Christmas has always been one of the saddest days of my life. Over the years, Gail went out of her way to try to make this a special day for me. She always wanted to make up for the many Christmases

I endured as a child with no gifts and no affection. Her efforts didn't always break through my holiday depression, but the gift she gave me in 1979 certainly did. That was the year she gave me a daughter for Christmas.

Gail and I tried to have a child for the first six years of our marriage with no luck. Finally, in January 1979, I saw a doctor looking for some explanation. He found that I had a low sperm count—most likely the result of high school wrestling days. During the football season, I stayed at 155 pounds; for wrestling, though, I had to drop down to 127 pounds. To help sweat off some of the weight, I spent hours in the hot tub after practice every day. This, the doctor said, is one of the worst things a man can do, potentially causing irreparable harm to his fertility. He prescribed some medication, but he offered no guarantees that Gail and I would ever be able to conceive.

A month later, just before my birthday on February 25, Gail came home and told me she had a wonderful birthday surprise for me. She cooked an amazing dinner and I could tell she was really excited as we ate. Finally, when we finished our meal, Gail handed me a card. I assumed it was my birthday card, but when I looked at it, my jaw dropped. It just had two little words written on it: "Congratulations, DAD!" I immediately burst into tears and wrapped my arms around her. I can't tell you how happy I was that day. But I don't believe for a minute that the doctor's prescription had anything to do with it. There's no way a few weeks on that medicine could have made such a radical change so quickly. No, this certainly had God's fingerprints all over it.

It sounds crazy, but Gail was pregnant in eleven of the twelve months of 1979, from late February until mid-December. Back then, we didn't know if we were having a boy or a girl, but I knew which one I wanted: a little girl. I was worried that I'd put too much pressure on a son to live up to the many things I'd accomplished. But a baby girl? I knew she'd melt my heart—and I was right.

Crystal Nicole March was born on December 16, 1979, and I discovered a love I'd never even imagined. Looking at my daughter, feeling her tiny hand squeeze my finger ... it put my own childhood in a whole new light. I don't know why my mother couldn't show any love to her children, but I knew in an instant my daughter would never know how that felt. To this day, one of my favorite pictures is one of Crystal and me dressed up and sitting together under the Christmas tree. God made up for a lifetime of missed Christmases with the greatest gift I ever could have hoped for: Crystal Nicole, my gift from heaven.

### A Loving Family at Last

Slowly but surely, Gail taught me by example what a loving family looked like, sounded like, and felt like. She took things to the next level after Crystal was born. My mother never cared whether I was happy or sad, but Gail made it her mission to make Crystal smile a hundred times a day. I never remember my mother hugging me once, but Gail gave Crystal a tight hug when she woke up and when she went to bed, and so many more in between. There was no way Gail would ever miss walking our daughter to her first day of school, forget her birthday, or withhold praise when it was deserved. It was all so different from my own upbringing, and I was so grateful that my daughter didn't have to grow up with the terrible sense of loneliness and emptiness that I had as a child. I credit that entirely to Gail.

In the end, the greatest gift Gail ever gave me was herself. There's no way I could have achieved all I have without her. In fact, I think she's the reason I'm still here today. If she had never been there to teach me to love, I probably would have dried up and withered away years ago.

## — CLIMBING THE RANKS —

I was almost twenty-three years old when we got married, and Gail was just ahead of me at twenty-four. At that point, I'd worked at Body by Fisher for one year as a regular employee and another eighteen months as an intern.

I threw myself into my work with a new sense of confidence, and I was rewarded for it. From 1973 to 1981, I didn't hold a single position for longer than six months. I was being promoted and molded by management by moving through different departments and gaining experience in all of them. And I loved it.

I don't think you'll find a successful black person around who isn't motivated by ugly stereotypes. You can bet I wanted to prove that a black man could be successful in a white man's world. And beyond that, I had put my past firmly in the past. I was no longer a child searching for love. I had all the love I needed in Gail. I was a husband and a professional with a tremendous job. I had the world by the tail. There were no roadblocks ahead of me and nothing to slow me down.

In 1979, I was granted my third patent, and I'd managed to rise through the ranks and was responsible for the design, development, and quality assurance of more than $3 billion in vehicle production parts and components. At that time at General Motors, there were eight possible levels of promotion an engineer could obtain before reaching the highest level of management, a category called *unclassified*. This was a level that only three percent of the engineers ever achieved in their careers.

*✳ UNCLASSIFIED ✳*

| JOB LEVEL | JOB DESCRIPTION |
|---|---|
| LEVEL 8 | TECHNICAL FELLOW / SENIOR MANAGER |
| LEVEL 7 | LEAD ENGINEER / ENGINEERING MANAGER |
| LEVEL 6 | SENIOR ENGINEER |
| LEVEL 5 | INTERMEDIATE ENGINEER |
| LEVEL 4 | JUNIOR ENGINEER |
| LEVEL 1–3 | ENTRY |

By twenty-seven, only four years after beginning my full-time employment at GM, I'd already reached the eighth level—one of the youngest engineers to hit that mark—and all that was left was for me to reach unclassified status.

I was promoted that year to chief engineer for the electric car at Body by Fisher. The electric car was a new idea on everyone's mind. The oil embargo of 1973 was in the recent past, and everyone could still picture the long lines at gas stations. So, like every other car manufacturer in the world at the time, GM brought all their divisions together to see what we could come up with. None of us realized at the time that it would take another thirty years before such a vehicle would actually go into production!

By this time in my career, I was at a crossroads. There was a separate classification for unique employees the company didn't want to promote into management. We called them Super 8. These employees were realizing their highest potential in their current department, and there was no reason to move them into management. It's like taking the best chef out of the kitchen and having him run the restaurant. It's a lose–lose. You want to keep your best people in their best seats. One such employee, the guy who worked right beside me, had 128 patents on seat belts! He was clearly in his sweet spot, and the company understandably did not want to move him up to management. He was best used staying there and flourishing.

Then there were the employees the company viewed as potential candidates for top management positions. They were known as executive prospects and were slated to become unclassified. It was from this pool of employees that the next top managers where selected, with the understanding that they had sufficient experience in each of the company's departments. In short order, I was transferred from the mechanical division to the sheet metal division, to plastics and the lab, all the while being encouraged and complimented by my higher-ups. They were clearly grooming me to become unclassified. Of course, this was flattering, but the most important aspect of being unclassified for me was that there was no longer a cap to how much you could earn.

One day in 1983, I walked into my boss's office to drop off a report, but he wasn't there. Right there on top of his desk, I saw a file with my name on it. I recognized it immediately as my personnel file. I wondered for a moment why he had my file out, but then I saw a note on the cover. It read, "Promote to unclassified. Move to Kokomo, Indiana."

I walked out of his office with mixed emotions. On one hand, any GM engineer would be thrilled to receive an unclassified rating. On the other hand, I'd been to Kokomo, and I had no desire to live there. Plus, we had a newborn at home and Gail had settled into a position at Honeywell that she really enjoyed. She had career ambitions of her own, and now I was supposed to ask her to leave her job and move to Indiana? All I had were questions with no answers. *What would Gail say about leaving Detroit? Would she find a job she enjoys as much and that offers the same career path? Would I be willing to move to Kokomo myself? Is this the right path for me, or should I try to stay put in my engineering role? What would my leaders say if I turned down the promotion? Would I have to leave GM and find another job?*

I wrestled with that decision for several days with no clear direction on what to do or where to go. Then, one day, the answer walked right into my office and literally fell on my desk.

## — TIME TO STEP UP ... OR STEP OUT —

I let the Kokomo opportunity simmer in the back of my mind for a little while and tried to keep my mind on my immediate responsibilities. That's what brought Chandler Lee, a fellow black engineer, into my office. He was seeking a letter of recommendation from a manager for his application to one of GM's lesser known programs. As a manager supervising fifty engineers, I was authorized and qualified to write such a letter, even though Chandler didn't work directly for me. He and I had gotten to know each other, and he thought I'd be the perfect person to recommend him for this opportunity.

After some small talk, I asked, "Chandler, what exactly are you applying for?"

"This," he said as he handed me a brochure. "It's the GM Minority Dealer Academy." I looked down at the booklet, scanned a few pages, and looked back up at him.

"Chandler," I said, "I've been working here for ten years, and I've never heard a single word about this Academy. What is it? What does it do?"

He explained that it was a fifteen-month, full-time, intensive study program that taught participants everything they needed to know about owning and operating a car dealership. Plus, during the entire program, the student received a full-time salary, health insurance, and a company car—all paid for by General Motors. It was designed to provide black entrepreneurs greater opportunity to own their own car dealerships, something that was all too rare in the late '70s and early '80s. In those days, almost all the dealerships were white-owned, and most of those were passed down generationally. On top of that, many of those dealerships still operated with a racially prejudiced attitude that prevented black professionals from having the chance to learn the trade and grow into management positions. The GM Minority Dealer Academy provided what well-qualified black entrepreneurs needed in the industry: the education, the hands-on instruction, and the chance to prove themselves.

I was fascinated by everything Chandler told me. The sting of being rushed out of Lloyd Cadillac and Buick as a child had never fully healed. Instead, it was a lasting image of how I saw the entire car dealership industry. In the decade I'd been working for GM, I didn't know a single black manager—let alone an owner—in a dealership anywhere in the country. But there was still one big question about the program.

"What happens when you complete the program?"
I asked. "How do graduates go from the academy and into
their own dealerships?"

He replied, "They search all over the country to see if they
can find a car dealership for you to buy."

"With what?" I asked. "Where would an academy graduate
get that kind of money?"

"That's the best part," Chandler said. "They've set up
a company called Motors Holding as a division of General
Motors. It lends you the money up front, interest free. Then,
you pay them back with part of the dealership's earnings
as you grow the business." He explained Motors Holding
would provide millions of dollars when necessary, with the
expectation that the borrower would repay the loan within
seven years. They'd then use that money again to provide loans
for other academy graduates.

I was impressed. Chandler had certainly done his
homework and showed real promise, so I didn't hesitate
to write his recommendation letter. But I couldn't get the
academy out of my head afterward. As I read through the
program's brochure and thought more about what Chandler
had said, I realized how innovative and groundbreaking it
was. The program provided a prospective owner with the
knowledge and insights to profitably run a dealership. But
without Motors Holding to provide financing to purchase a
dealership, the education would have been all but wasted. Most
black people just didn't have the financial backing to purchase
a dealership, and it could still be difficult for a black man to

procure such a large loan from a traditional bank. Adequate knowledge and funding were the two biggest stumbling blocks to owning a dealership, and this program was the solution to both.

> **Most black people just didn't have the financial backing to purchase a dealership.**

The thought of owning a car dealership was tremendously appealing. I was an entrepreneur at heart, and Gail and I had often talked about how great it would be to own our own business. We had even considered buying an electronics company months earlier, but we ultimately decided to pass on the deal. Then, just as I was facing a big decision about my future with GM, this unexpected opportunity came along. It was hard not to see this as an answer to all my questions and the start of the greatest adventure of my life.

It wasn't all upside, though. As much as I liked the idea of working for myself, I knew it would be risk to leave a steady, secure, good-paying job at GM to chase a dream with no guarantee of success. Not every academy graduate ended up with a dealership or had the qualifications to secure a Motors Holding loan. My salary at that time was $60,000. It was a solid income that would be reduced by more than half, down to $24,000 annually, if I entered the academy. I would also lose all my GM stock options, then valued at $100,000—an amount that was unthinkable back in the Black Box. And then there was the issue of moving. I knew that if I was fortunate enough to get through the academy, secure a loan, and succeed in buying a dealership, I would have to uproot my family and move wherever we found a good dealership opportunity. Of course, if I stayed with GM, I'd have to move to Indiana sooner rather than later, so it looked like our days in Detroit were numbered anyway.

My head was spinning with questions and possibilities, and I needed Gail's input before I let my mind wander any further. I worried she'd think I was crazy to consider giving up the successful career I'd built just to chase a new dream. Many wives might have done that, but not Gail. She thought about the options for a while and then said, "I've seen you working fifteen hours a day as an engineer, and I know you'll do the same with this. If you want to go for it, you've got my support. Besides, this new venture won't suck the engineering knowledge out of your brain. If the Dealer Academy doesn't work out or if no ownership possibilities come your way, you can always go back to being an engineer. That's a pretty good backup plan."

Her faith in me was just the encouragement I needed to take the leap. I talked to my boss soon after and sent in my own application for the academy. A few weeks later, when my acceptance letter arrived in the mail, I thought a lot about the twists and turns my life had taken to get me to this point. There were times I wanted to give up, times when I felt like I was all alone and no one cared whether I won or lost. In those seasons, the only thing that kept me going was a burning desire to do more, to *be* more. I always knew God had big things in store for me; now I prayed I was right about this next step in that plan.

Providence had brought me this far, and I was trusting it to take me to the next level. If Chandler Lee hadn't walked into my office for that letter of recommendation, I wouldn't have taken this abrupt turn toward entrepreneurship. It was the same as when I found Moses Johnson from Howard University waiting for me in the tiny living room of my Black Box house, and the same as when I got back to work after a disappointing college graduation to find the girl of my dreams sitting at my desk. Opportunity had come looking for me once again, and I was ready for it.

Just a few weeks later, I said goodbye to my colleagues and packed up my desk after more than a decade at Body by Fisher. It was time for the hardworking student to go back to school.

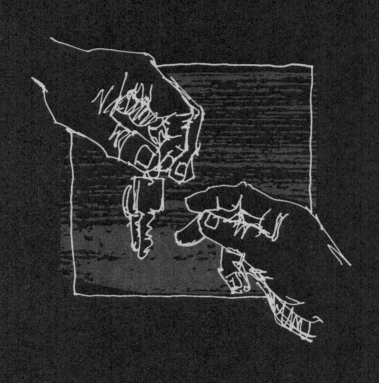

# FIVE

## Making My Mark on the Car Business

"Nothing is impossible. The word
itself says, 'I'm possible!'"

~ AUDREY HEPBURN ~

In the early 1970s, minorities represented about thirteen percent of the nation's population, and many of them were car owners. But there were only a few black auto dealers in the entire United States. In the "Motor City" of Detroit—where a majority of factory workers purchased GM cars—there wasn't a single black car dealer. You had to wonder what the heck was going on. Eventually, pressure mounted to increase the number of minority dealers. In 1972, Ford started the ball rolling by creating a program to help minority citizens learn the skills required to successfully run a car dealership. They were followed by Chrysler and then GM, which, of course, is where I learned the ropes.

A decade later, by the mid-1980s, black dealership owners were finally becoming more common. I'd love to say they all experienced remarkable success, but I can't. It's a challenging business for *anyone*—especially owners who had to face the uphill battle of ongoing prejudice, a tough economy, and endlessly fighting for a seat at the table. These struggles became my whole world in 1984, however, and I was determined to turn every challenge into a profitable opportunity. I knew I could make it as a car dealer ... but even I never imagined how much my life was about to change.

## — THE GM MINORITY DEALER ACADEMY —

How do you train someone to own and oversee a successful car dealership in fifteen months? Better yet, how do you accomplish the task when a third of your students—like me—have never even worked in a car dealership before? The answer is *immersion*. The academy threw us into the deep end on day one, giving students the chance to eat, sleep, and breathe the industry every single day. It was boot camp for car dealers, and it was intense.

I began at the GM Minority Dealer Academy in June 1984. The program alternated between one month of full-time, daily classroom instruction and ninety days of actual hands-on experience at a dealership, observing and putting into practice what we learned in class. The first third of our training focused on the new and used car departments of a dealership, the second portion on parts and service, and the final segment on accounting practices that are critical to financial success.

I took my dealership schooling and assignments just as seriously as I took my high school and college education. After a day of classes, while my fifteen classmates were drinking and socializing downstairs in the bar, I was up in my hotel room studying accounting practices in the car business. Fifteen-hour days were the norm, not the exception. When a dealer couldn't take the time to show me what I needed to know, I'd visit the department and staff who did the work and learn directly from them. I was determined to learn *everything* about the car business during my time in the academy—even when small-minded jerks got in my way.

## Hot Dogs and Small Minds

The biggest problem of the program involved the ninety-day segments in the real world of auto sales, service, and financial operations. We were placed with car dealers across the country who had partnered with the academy. The idea was that the student would shadow the dealer and his managers to see how they managed the day-to-day operations of the business. This would give the student a front-row seat to just about any issue that might come up while owning and operating a dealership. This, of course, required the active cooperation of the dealers we were assigned to. When the dealer was excited about and plugged into the program, things went great; it was a perfect way to learn. The dealers benefited, too, because the academy paid them for their participation *and* the dealer received free labor from the students during the ninety-day rotation. It was a win-win. Except when it wasn't.

Sadly, not all the dealers were interested in creating a helpful learning environment. Even worse, some of them clearly didn't like the idea of minority car dealers at all. That attitude was good incentive for me. I learned to take the high road in interpersonal encounters and used their prejudice as motivation to succeed. I'd be lying if I said it was always easy, though. In fact, the closest I've ever come to a physical fight in my life happened right there on a mentor-dealer's lot. The sales manager, a guy named David, showed a clear disdain for the opportunity I'd been given and questioned why a black man should get a shot at a dealership. We didn't get along, but I kept things professional until he finally pushed things too far. I showed up for work one day expecting to review critical financial and sales procedures with David as planned. Instead, he sent me outside—dressed in a suit and tie—to cook hot dogs and hamburgers for customers.

It should be clear by now that I'm not above doing any kind of work. There's

> **Not all the dealers were interested in creating a helpful learning environment. Even worse, some of them clearly didn't like the idea of minority car dealers at all.**

absolutely nothing wrong with having an employee cook
hot dogs and hamburgers for customers. The problem
was, that's not why I was there. I wasn't there as a regular
employee; I was there as a future owner to be educated on
the executive-level operations of the business. And here
was a bigoted sales manager, who clearly didn't want me
there, trying to pull a power play by making me stand
outside behind a grill all day. It was the last straw with this
guy. I told him I wasn't going to do it.

David called his superior to complain about my
"insubordination." I explained I was there to learn the car
business, not to cook hot dogs. While David was ranting to
his boss, I called one of the top GM executives who ran the
academy and told him what was going on. He was livid. He
called the dealership immediately and asked David, "Why
exactly do you want our academy student out there cooking
hot dogs?" Needless to say, I didn't end up cooking any hot
dogs that day . . . or any day after.

Looking back, I think that's the maddest I've ever been
in my life. But I turned the entire situation to my advantage.
Throughout my life, my success has been built on what I call
the "little people," the small minority of people with closed
minds and big prejudices. In this case, I used David's behavior
toward me as fuel. He made me want to succeed in my quest
more than ever!

As a quick aside, let me jump ahead to when I finally
opened my first car dealership. I sent out invitations to our
grand opening celebration, and I hand wrote the first invitation

myself. I addressed it to David. I wanted to make sure it was delivered right into his own hands. Since then, I've always told people not to let the "little people" bring them down. Instead, you can use them as your inspiration to do more and go further just to prove them wrong.

## Closing the Deal

By the time we finished the education portion of program in May 1985, I was confident I could successfully run a car dealership. The real challenge was buying one in the first place. Not every graduate was guaranteed a dealership. In my class of fifteen graduates, for example, only three received offers in the first year. That was typical, as only 30 percent of all academy graduates actually ended up owning a car dealership. And of the academy graduates who did get dealerships, only half of them were able to pay back their Motors Holding loan in the agreed-upon seven-year period.

There were several reasons for these lackluster results. For example, most of the dealerships up for grabs to minority dealers were already failing businesses. They had serious financial issues and were located in undesirable locations. Dealership owners who ran successful businesses rarely wanted to sell. Why would they? For a while, the only dealerships available to academy graduates were those being sold by white owners who wanted to get out of areas that had turned into ghettos.

With all that in the back of my mind, we were each asked

to give a twenty-minute presentation to General Motors' top five manufacturer representatives, all of whom wanted to know why they should give a dealership to us. Each graduate tried to convince the executives that he would be a successful dealership owner. I based my presentation on my résumé and an executive summary of what I'd accomplished. Some fellow graduates used slides, while others used testimonial letters. We each did our best, but nobody knew if any offers would come in. All we could do was wait.

## — TONY MARCH BUICK —

I didn't have to wait long. As it turned out, I was the first in my class to get a dealership offer. I got a call from Bob Colletta of Buick Motor Company. He said, "Tony, we want you to fly up to look at this dealership in Hartford, Connecticut." I was excited, but I was aware of something they called "dealer-itis," when graduates got so desperate to become owners that they bought the first dealership that came along—even if it had little chance of succeeding. I was determined to not make that mistake. I did my due diligence by speaking with city officials in Hartford and the people at Motors Holding about their assessment of the dealership's potential. I even anonymously visited the dealership to get a feel for how the place was run and the quality of its employees.

The dealership, Pearce Buick, had a bad reputation for

losing money. In fact, it hadn't turned a profit in at least five years. Not exactly a business I was excited to purchase, but I had seen the company's employees in action and studied the actuarial projections and population statistics. I was confident that by instituting some changes, I could turn the dealership around and make a profit. I took out a seven-year loan for $2.3 million from Motors Holding, and Tony March Buick opened in September of 1985 in Hartford. I was on my way.

## Quick Turnaround

I'll cut to the chase and say up front that we were able to turn the dealership's downward trend around faster than anyone predicted. Within six months, we were out of the red and had turned a half-million-dollar profit. Yes, we did it quickly, but it certainly wasn't easy. Once I got into the nitty gritty of the business, though, I saw that the academy had taught me everything I needed to know to succeed. I also realized that the existing employees wanted to win; they just needed help learning how to get there and how to achieve a sense of satisfaction and pride in their work. Throw in a whole lot of hard work and plenty of long hours, and you get the successful Tony March Buick of Hartford.

I was fortunate in those first several months because there was nothing to distract me from my job. Gail and Crystal hadn't moved to Hartford yet, and I stayed in an apartment—a terrible place with prostitutes and drug dealers wandering around. The sketchy neighbors didn't bother me, though; all I did there was sleep. I didn't have to worry about cutting the lawn, maintaining a home, caring for family, or keeping social obligations. I lived and breathed the dealership from the first day I purchased it.

My pace was crazy, even for me. For the first six months, I worked at the dealership seventeen hours a day. Gail called me every night at midnight from our home in Michigan to tell me to go home. I did what she said, because I had to be back the next day at 7:00 a.m. when the service department opened.

I had critical demographic information about Hartford, and I poured over the dealership's numbers to pinpoint why it was losing money. Working with my Motors Holding rep, we agreed if I could sell eighty more cars a month—increasing monthly car sales from 100 to 180—the dealership would be profitable. I was convinced I could do this. I knew other Buick dealerships with locations and buyer profiles similar to my own that had achieved that number.

> **Gail called me every night at midnight from our home in Michigan to tell me to go home.**

I soon realized the main problem wasn't the market; it was management. The eighty-three-year-old owner I was replacing was not a hands-on kind of guy. When he ran the place, he showed up three times a week for lunch with the general manager, a man who clearly wasn't doing a good job. Also, I could easily identify several places in the operation where we could save and/or earn more money. There was plenty of room for improvement. My main job, though, was gaining the employees' trust and convincing them—from the general manager down—to adopt my new workplace policies. It'd be a shock to their system, but I knew it could work. I just had to get them all on board.

I set my plans in motion the very first day I walked into the dealership. I gathered everyone together, introduced myself, and said, "As your new owner, I guarantee that no one in this dealership will be terminated in the first three months. Each of you will have the chance to prove yourself. I'm a trained engineer, a graduate of GM's Minority Dealer Academy, and I've done every job you're doing here, from washing cars and servicing in the back to selling and financing up front. I know we can make this work. Money is not an issue here as it has been in the past. I'm going to spend money to spruce this place up so customers will feel comfortable buying and servicing their cars here. We have the financial resources to make payroll and turn a profit. And when we start making money—and I am confident we will—each of you will share in the benefits through better job security and a bigger paycheck."

Over the next sixty days, I spent an additional $60,000 and some serious sweat equity to keep my promise of making the dealership more attractive to prospective customers. I wanted to show the employees that not only would I keep my word when I made a promise, but that I was also committed to turning

things around. Plus, I wanted them to see firsthand
that the days of having a distant, hands-off owner were
over. The entire team quickly learned that no one in
the organization would work harder, longer, or more
passionately than their new boss.

Only one employee left the dealership in my first three
months of operation. How and why he lost his job says
a lot about the faith my employees were willing to place
in me. The man had written the N-word on the wall of
the technicians' bathroom. Rather than support his racial
prejudice, his fellow workers actually came to me and
reported what he had done. I didn't even have to fire the
guy; he quit when he found out his
coworkers had turned him in.

That situation gave me a
huge swell of encouragement.
I saw that the employees
felt confident in what I
was doing. After working
years for a boss who had allowed the
dealership to go downhill, they were
watching me and thinking, *This is a guy
who can turn things around.* Almost everyone
in a dealership worked on commission, so they understood
what they could gain from being loyal to a leader who had
the determination to face a failing business and turn it into a
profitable one.

## A Plan for Success

By the end of that first year, we had turned a failing dealership that was bleeding cash into a thriving business with a healthy bottom line. The team at Tony March Buick had done a fantastic job, and I couldn't have been prouder of them. In the years after this successful turnaround, especially as I mentored other new and potential dealership owners, I was often asked how I managed to pull off such a dramatic shift in one year's time. I can break it down into seven easy steps.

First, as I mentioned, I started by encouraging my employees. By promising not to terminate anyone for the first few months, I gave them some breathing room. The team didn't take this commitment for granted. They were well aware that many ownership transitions immediately lead to a string of firings. By taking that fear off their shoulders, I was able to provide them with a sense of security and strong motivation to prove their worth to the business.

Second, I volunteered my own time and money to upgrade the physical appearance of the dealership, making it a more attractive draw for customers. This not only made the place look and feel nicer, it also encouraged the rest of the team to show some pride in their workplace themselves.

Third, I established a relationship with the media. After all, I was the first black car dealer in Hartford. It was a big achievement, and I knew I could leverage it into free publicity. It worked. The local media outlets got on board and produced several articles and TV news features that helped promote the dealership.

Fourth, I put procedures in place to increase visits to the service department. This is something the previous owner completely neglected, and it cost him dearly. The service department should be an incredible revenue stream for any dealership. If it's not, something is seriously wrong. To get things moving, I started sending out reminder notices to all former customers, reminding them when their three-thousand-mile oil change was due. The cost of the postcards was peanuts compared to the revenue this brought in. It reminded car owners that they could get their oil changed at the same place they bought their cars—and who knew more about their car than the dealership?

I also offered new buyers free oil changes for life and a weekly complimentary car wash. No other dealer in Hartford was offering that kind of deal. Buyers saw it as a huge incentive; I did too. This brought cars back to the dealership for service on a regular basis, giving technicians the chance to inspect the car for other necessary services. This also gave us a chance to let customers know about the manufacturer's suggested maintenance, such as the routine fifty-thousand-mile inspection that most people never remember to do.

Keeping a constant flow of customers coming through the service center had another obvious benefit: it brought them into our showroom. While waiting on their car to be serviced or repaired, many people passed the time by wandering around the showroom checking out the new models. I can't tell you how many sales we got by attracting this kind of captive audience! Besides, once we got car owners used to coming onto our lot for service, it was perfectly natural for them to come to us when it was time to buy a new car.

Fifth, I changed the mix of products and pricing in the parts department. Before my time, the Pearce Buick parts department grossed 26 percent on sales, trailing behind comparable dealerships that averaged 31 percent. By increasing traffic to the service center, we increased our need for parts. The trick at that point was to price those parts to maximize profits without overcharging the customer.

I carefully studied successful parts departments of several other dealerships and changed our pricing across the board. I knew we couldn't and shouldn't jack up the prices on things like oil changes (that didn't qualify for our free offer) and tires because the customer would notice those increases immediately. All they had to do was compare our prices to Jiffy Lube or one of the dozen other tire stores. However, customers are less sensitive to price increases under the hood. A price increase on an alternator wouldn't be as noticeable as higher prices on tires, so we concentrated on those areas. Of course, we never gouged customers by sneaking unreasonable costs into any repair; we simply raised the price of some services where we had been undercharging, dropped the price on some services where we had been overcharging, and left the price alone on services that were doing well. It was just a basic price adjustment, something the previous owner inexplicably hadn't done in several years.

Sixth, I stopped loss of revenue due to employee dishonesty.

This was a tough one, and it became a huge issue for me because I realized my general manager and used car manager were both getting kickbacks from wholesalers. They'd sell a used car from my lot to a wholesaler for less than the expected price, and then the wholesaler would give them $500 cash as a thank-you. My guys also paid more for cars at auction than they should have, again scoring a $500 bonus for themselves on each car. Once I figured out what was happening, I put systems in place to stop it immediately. Instead of outright accusing my employees of ripping me off, I simply told them I needed to sign off on all used cars being bought or sold. That ended the kickback problem and returned thousands of dollars to the dealership's bottom line.

**Instead of being stuck with six-speed white Buicks that wouldn't sell, I ordered grey Buicks with eight cylinders and they flew off the lot.**

Seventh and last, I increased new car sales by stocking the showroom with popular models. When I took over the dealership, I was left with an inventory of cars no one wanted. I knew immediately that I had to get rid of all that useless stock and replace it with the hottest Buicks on the market. During my internship at another Buick dealership, I had learned about a company newsletter called the "What's Hot" booklet that showcased the best-selling models. My new team didn't even know such a resource existed. I based my new car orders on it and quickly turned over the stock in my showroom. Instead of being stuck with six-speed white Buicks that wouldn't sell, I ordered grey Buicks with eight cylinders and they flew off the lot.

None of these strategies was rocket science, but they were all I needed to stem the bleeding at a failing dealership and turn it into thriving business. Things kept getting better and better at Tony March Buick, and I was even able to repay my seven-year, $2.3 million Motors Holding loan in just thirty-three months—more than four years early. They told me it was one of the quickest repayments in the Motors Holding's history.

I was happy, Motors Holding was happy, General Motors was happy, and my employees were definitely happy. I knew going into the business that the best way to change the mind-set of my team members was to increase the amount of their paychecks. These were men and women who'd been through Pearce Buick's bad days, worrying if their former owner would even be able to make payroll each week. This was a good team working under a bad coach, and they were grateful for the leadership change. I knew it was working several months in when Rick, the service manager, looked at his ever-increasing paycheck and said, "Oh, Tony, where have you been all my life?"

## A Giving Problem

The success we enjoyed turning the Buick dealership around was wonderful, but it did not make us immune to the auto recession of the late '80s. Our business took a hit, just like every other car dealership in the country. In fact, Tony March Buick didn't turn a profit at all in 1989. Fortunately, I had already paid off my Motors Holding loan early and had saved up enough financial reserves to weather the storm. I thought we'd be okay … until my accountant brought me an unexpected problem: I was in danger of an IRS audit.

My crime? I was giving too much money away. Ever since my college days, doing community service with Alpha Phi Omega, I'd had a passion for helping other people. I gave what little I could during the first decade of my career with GM, but my giving took a big upswing once I paid off my Motors Holding loan. I identified several charities I wanted to support and had started donating large sums to those causes. Even when we made no profit in 1989, I still donated a good percentage of our revenue to them. Apparently, this is a red flag for the IRS.

**My accountant explained, "Your charitable donations are really high, but the business is only breaking even."**

My accountant explained, "Your charitable donations are really high, but the business is only breaking even. The federal government is going to wonder why a person who's not *making* any money would *give* so much money to charity." I didn't know what to say. The idea that the federal government would penalize me for supporting worthwhile causes was a shock to my system. It was an early lesson in having to figure out a good, legal process for doing the giving I'd always wanted

to do. I just never imagined the government would try to
stop me from helping people.

— ADDING SATURN: GM'S NEW DARLING —

By 1991, I was struggling with two big problems: the
sluggish auto economy and the continuing decay of my
dealership's area. It was becoming a bit of a slum. The
type of people who could afford a Buick didn't live there or
even want to visit. They took their business to the "better" parts
of town. I could hardly blame them. I mean, it's a bad idea to
put a McDonald's in a vegetarian neighborhood! You've got to
know your market, and my market had moved out of the area.

I tried for years to swap or buy some property to move
my dealership to a more sales-favorable area. Finally, in 1992,
the city agreed to sell me a parcel of land at the exit ramp of
a major interstate highway, a location where tens of thousands
of cars passed by daily. I sold my own building and land to
someone who turned it into a car parts store and body shop.
It was a perfect fit for the neighborhood. People there didn't
buy cars; they fixed what they had. Now they had a place to
buy the parts they needed.

My good fortune didn't end with a better dealership
location. A new kind of car—and car company—had just hit
the market. Saturn, built by a subsidiary of GM, exploded
onto the car scene and became enormously popular among
car buyers. The appeal wasn't just the look and quality of the

vehicles; it was the entire purchasing experience. Saturn was laser-focused on providing an excellent customer experience, and they were extremely picky when it came to who they allowed to represent their brand. They wanted dealers with a proven track record, so only dealers with superior customer service were awarded dealerships. That's why I was so proud to be awarded one of the first twenty-four Saturn dealerships in the country. It spoke volumes about how the industry saw what we had been doing at Tony March Buick.

I had the chance to put on my engineering hat and got involved in the construction of the new dealership from the ground up on my new piece of land. Motors Holding gave me another loan, which I repaid in less than twenty-four months. I believed it was better to get those loans paid off sooner than later, so I could get that money working for me. Motors Holding tells me I still hold the record as the only car dealer to satisfy four separate Motors Holding loans, all in less time than the required seven years.

The new March Buick-Saturn dealership opened in February 1993. It was a gala event that brought several VIPs to Hartford, including the GM Chairman Jack Smith with the heads of four of GM's five divisions. We also hosted Governor Lowell Weicker, Jr., Mayor Carrie Saxon Perry, a few congressmen, and all the major news outlets. It was a big day for the city and an even bigger one for me.

In its first eleven months of operation, the dealership made $2 million. Over the next four years, we saw a 500 percent increase in sales and generated the highest return on sales—more than 9 percent—of any Saturn dealership in the country. By comparison, the average dealership nationally made a 2 percent return on sales during the same time period. I can't take all the credit, though. A large part of my success was Saturn's popularity right out of the gate. Buyers especially loved the fact that there was no price haggling with a Saturn. Every buyer paid the same price for their vehicles everywhere in the country. That was the hook, and people loved it.

Saturn changed the way dealers did business. Because Saturn salespeople were paid by the hour instead of on commission—a first in the industry—there was no sales pressure with customers. Instead, the salesperson could spend their time educating the car buyer on the car itself, rather than spending ten minutes talking about the car and three hours negotiating a price. Plus, the car was inherently cheaper to produce because it was small, and Saturn offered just two basic models and three interior option packages. A new factory was built, specifically designed to produce the Saturn more efficiently and with improved quality control. It included more robotics, teams instead of individuals on the assembly line, and all the parts required under one roof.

It was incredible. In the beginning, having a Saturn dealership was like minting money. The cars were so popular that they were either presold when they arrived or they were snapped up within a few days. That saved on our floor-plan costs, the money a dealer has to pay the bank for all its unsold inventory. The popularity of Saturn and the fact that every dealer charged the same price also meant I could risk spending less on advertising than my competitors. Everyone else was spending $30,000 a month on marketing, so I tried just spending $10,000. I figured the other dealers could advertise the price and features of the product, and then I'd just let people know they could buy a Saturn from us. My plan worked, and that alone resulted in nearly a quarter-million-dollar savings every year that went right back to my bottom line.

I also watched my expenses in staffing, finding I actually got higher productivity from fewer employees. When I had three people do the work of four, for example, I gave half those savings to the remaining three employees and kept the other half for the dealership. When Saturn took over the inventory control and parts shipping, I realized I no longer needed a parts manager. I had the service manager take over both functions and gave him a 25 percent raise, keeping the other 75 percent savings for the dealership. This was such an obvious cost-cutting opportunity that I was surprised when other Saturn dealers didn't do it. With these and a few other tweaks, I brought my average personnel costs down to 24 percent of my budget compared to the average dealer's personnel cost of 39 percent.

All these things helped, but I really think the main reason for our success was our constant focus on superior customer service. Remember, the reason I was awarded a Saturn dealership in the first place was the excellent reputation we had among our clients. If it ain't broke, don't fix it!

The thing is, anyone can sell a person one car. The

secret is to sell them *five* cars. You don't sell them five cars based on sales price; it's how you treat them after the first sale. That's why I encouraged my salespeople to build strong relationships with their customers. A good salesperson should serve as a trusted friend who can be relied upon, with occasional phone calls to check in and quick responses when a customer reaches out. This approach sold more cars and cut down on employee turnover, a widespread problem in the car industry. Employees don't want to leave a dealership if they can rely on repeat business from satisfied customers.

**The thing is, anyone can sell a person one car. The secret is to sell them *five* cars.**

I can't overstate the importance of Saturn to my long-term success. On the heels of a major slump in the automobile industry, the explosive success of Saturn helped take my business further than I ever imagined in just a few years. More importantly, the success I had with that first dealership gave me a solid business reputation and financial foundation I needed to help other dealers who were facing much harder times than I was.

## — FIGHTING FOR MINORITY CAR DEALERS —

Despite the success my team and I were having during those years, I had to acknowledge that other minority entrepreneurs were still struggling to own car dealerships and turn a profit. I understood them, their struggles, and the pressure to achieve. I wanted to reach back and help them along.

In the early '80s, less than one hundred of General Motors' 10,000 dealers across the country were black. It became clear the best way to increase the success of black dealerships was by doing it the way white dealers had since the 1920s: form a council to meet with the GM chairman directly to voice their opinions and concerns. So, the General Motors Black Dealer Advisory Council was created in 1983. It became more inclusive of other manufacturers and was renamed the Minority Dealer Advisory Council in 1988. I was elected chairman that year and stayed in the role for thirteen years, its longest-serving chairman. In that role, I met with the president of GM every quarter. At the same time, a group of colleagues and I founded the independent GM Minority Dealers Association, hoping to improve business opportunities for all. I served as president of that organization from 1990 to 1992.

By the late '80s, things had reached critical mass. A downturn in the car-buying market meant even strong dealerships were struggling to stay afloat. Dealers with fewer resources were failing at an alarming rate. Of course, the largest proportion of failures were black dealers saddled with the most undesirable dealerships to start with, leaving them without the means to weather an economic storm.

It was a tough time for the industry and for me personally. Every time a minority member lost a dealership, it came across my desk because I was serving as chairman of the council. Dealers were calling me, begging me to help them

save their dealerships. Emotionally, it was some of the worst
years of my life, seeing all those families destroyed. During
those years, I was spending five hours in a week on Tony
March Buick and sixty-five on the minority dealer issue.
I did what I could, often appealing to Motors Holding to
give dealers additional loans, longer payback periods, or
reduced monthly loans. At best, it was a stopgap measure that
slowed the rate of minority dealership failures, but it did help
individuals here and there.

In 1988, forty-four minority dealers out of a total of 210
went out of business. The next year, forty-nine more waved the
white flag. In just those two years, almost
50 percent of minority dealers went under.

Racism certainly didn't make things
easier. It paid to know the right people to
get a premium location, and black dealers
weren't given a fair shake. At the time, a
joke circulated in the black community that
you had to give the Honda zone manager a
Rolex to even have a shot at getting a Honda
dealership. In fact, a famous dealer with
NASCAR ties was eventually convicted of
giving kickbacks to executives for preferential consideration.
And really, why would a zone manager give a dealership to a
black dealer when he had three or four rich white guys who
wanted it and were willing to offer kickbacks—things much
bigger and better than a watch?

Only the GM chairman could make sure minority dealers

> **In just those two years, almost 50 percent of minority dealers went under. Racism certainly didn't make things easier.**

weren't getting shortchanged in their efforts to own desirable dealerships. He could demand zone managers to stop their under-the-table deals and exclusionary practices. As the spokesperson for minority dealers, I'd appealed to management for years to make the call.

Finally, in 1991, our efforts paid off. A law firm in Washington, D.C., was hired to determine the biases of how dealerships were awarded and made a list of more than two hundred recommendations to make things right. The GM president at the time, Lloyd Reuss, publicly announced the company would increase minority dealers by 40 percent. As chairman of the council, I had the honor of signing an agreement with GM to memorialize this pledge. Incredible! It was a turning point. The playing field for minority and white dealers was finally being leveled.

I spent thousands of volunteer hours fighting to stem the flow of black dealership bankruptcies and convincing GM to increase the number of minority owners. Looking back, I can rest comfortably, knowing I did my part. As I climbed the car dealership mountain, I reached back and pulled up others. I didn't save everyone, but I did the best I could.

For all that hard work, I was given the GM Minority Dealer Association's Trailblazer Award in 2007. Receiving the award was certainly satisfying, but the real sense of accomplishment came from knowing I helped so many other dealers keep their businesses afloat. Paying it backward, not money or awards, is what keeps me going. It allows me to see how far I've come, it points me forward on my path, and it validates my mission to serve "the least of these" as Matthew 25:40, one of my favorite Bible verses, calls us to do—and which I'll talk more about in another chapter.

## — GROWING AND GIVING —

Most car dealers own one dealership in their lifetime. Owning two or more is rare. In 2008, I was operating twenty-one dealerships in seven states. They ranged from moderate-priced American cars to the most expensive imports. That year, there were thirty-four auto manufacturers selling cars in the United States, and throughout my automotive career I had signed as dealership owner with twenty-one of them.

It was a busy time. I built seventeen of my dealerships from the ground up. In one year, I was building seven dealerships in six different states, racking up two hundred airplane trips in one year. I also had the opportunity during those years to act as a mentor. For example, Honda flew me out to California to address one hundred dealers about how to open a successful and profitable dealership. I always loved those opportunities to pay it backward by offering my encouragement and giving others the benefit of my experience.

Over the years, I've been honored to receive thirty-two

distinguished car dealer awards, including *Black Enterprise* magazine's Auto Dealer of the Year (in 1999 and 2013) and *TIME* magazine's Quality Dealer Award (in 1996 and 2007). The *TIME* awards meant a lot; it's generally considered the top award in my industry, kind of like an actor winning an Academy Award. I especially like the fact that the main factor *TIME* considered was the dealer's charitable contributions to his community. That's always been something I've tried to do both as a private individual and as a business owner. In fact, I was recognized in 1996 by *TIME* as one of the top ten most philanthropic dealers—out of 22,000 possible candidates—in America.

In 1998, I joined forces with another black car dealer, Ernie Hodge, to form the March/Hodge Holding Company. Just five years later, we were recognized by *Black Enterprise* magazine as the fifth largest black-owned business in America and placed first in its ranking of top minority dealerships in the country. We've managed to maintain the first or second spot on that list in all the years since.

— **WHAT GOES AROUND COMES AROUND** —

experienced another victory in 1998, a personal victory I honestly never saw coming. Earlier in this book, I mentioned how my brothers and I sold *Grit* magazine on a two-mile sales route every Saturday in the Daytona heat. You'll remember that we often tried to use the water fountain located in the showroom of Lloyd Cadillac and Buick, but the employees there chased us out every time. In our heat and desperation, we had to sneak around back to drink from the dirty water hose the crew used to wash the dealer's cars. I never forgot how it felt to not be "good enough" to walk through a dealership showroom. I often thought about it as I strolled through my own showrooms years later. That experience left a scar on me as a young boy that all my success still hadn't fully healed.

You know what they say, though: what goes around comes around. Well, it was time for Lloyd Cadillac and Buick to come back around. In August 1998, my new partner, Ernie, called and asked if I wanted to buy a Cadillac dealership. I asked him where it was located, and he said, "Let's see ... it's in Daytona Beach, Florida. You know it?"

"Yes," I replied. "I know it very well." There was only one Cadillac dealership in Daytona Beach. It was the one that chased me out of the showroom every week. It was the one I wasn't good enough to walk into. It was the one that made me drink from a dirty hose out back. It was Lloyd Cadillac and Buick. And it was for sale. A smile thirty years in coming spread across my face as I said, "Ernie, I'll take it."

In 1998, we purchased the dealership with our $750,000 and a new Motors Holding loan. We got in there, cleaned things up, turned the business around, and sold it eight years later ... for $25 million. Not bad for a kid who wasn't able to even grace the threshold of the place thirty years earlier.

And what about Willie, the kind black car washer who

saved my brothers and me from dehydration by allowing us to drink from the hose? Would you believe he still worked there? He had been there for forty-two years when I bought the place. Everyone knew ole Willie; he was a staple of the Black Box community. He even had a side business washing cars on his own every Saturday and Sunday on the streets I used to wander as a child. I flew down there soon after buying the dealership to meet the employees and introduce myself, and there he was. I didn't even recognize him at first, but he recognized me. He remembered those Saturdays when he helped the young, overheated entrepreneurs by giving us a drink.

Willie had worked for a white boss his entire life, so, when he heard a black man had bought the dealership, he was shocked. When he realized it was me—someone who had grown up on those same tough streets, a black man who had escaped the Black Box and found the kind of success the locals believed to be impossible—he was over the moon. I think Willie was prouder of me in that moment than anyone has ever been. Seeing him that day, going back "home" and talking to him...it was one of the best days of my life. No award I've ever won has meant more to me than the pride that beamed out of his eyes for what I'd accomplished.

> **Willie had worked for a white boss his entire life, so, when he heard a black man had bought the dealership ... he was over the moon.**

I appreciated the automotive business. It was fast-paced with lots of opportunity, and by 2008, I had achieved greater success than I could've ever believed possible. I was so happy that my business gave me a way to get involved in Hartford's civic projects and charities. Plus, it gave me a platform to launch charitable campaigns and a way to get other people excited about helping those who are living difficult lives. All that hustle allowed me to pay it backward to the people and communities I knew so well: the poor, the abused, the vulnerable.

And I was just getting started.

# SIX

---

## Investing in Education

---

*"Education is the most*
*powerful weapon which you*
*can use to change the world."*

~ NELSON MANDELA ~

lived and worked in Hartford for nearly twenty-five years. All during that time, I never stopped hustling. I was busy building a multimillion-dollar business, helping other minority car dealers across the country, and fighting for change in an old industry that was set in its ways. Beyond that, I took on a lot of other business and civic responsibilities, including cofounding a bank and serving as the director of American Leadership Forum and the Better Business Bureau. I also got involved in the sports industry, eventually establishing and leading the Hartford Sports and Entertainment Group, which brought professional basketball and arena football teams to Hartford. I was even co-owner of a group that came within twenty-four hours of purchasing the New England Patriots—that was a real nail-biter. And I spent a long time as commissioner of the Capital City Economic Development Authority, which was charged with spending a billion dollars to revitalize the city of Hartford.

That was a nail-biter of a different kind. I'll talk about that later.

Along the way, I racked up a lot of awards and honors. Those are always nice, and I appreciated each one. But I was also careful not to let myself get consumed by business and busyness. Once I got to the point that I knew my family was taken care of and that we'd never have to worry about going hungry, I never really cared about making money for money's sake. For me, business has always been the basis for giving back. So, as my career expanded, I realized it was time to move beyond writing checks. I could see that the financial resources, public recognition, and credibility I'd gained as a successful entrepreneur were simply tools I could use to help other people. After years of struggle followed by years of hard work and success, I was now in a much better position to make a significant difference in the lives of the less fortunate.

I'll say up front, though, that it's a little strange for me to spend a few chapters chronicling the things I've done to help people over the years. I did most of my giving in secret and spent years avoiding the spotlight. However, as I'll explain later in this book, some friends convinced me to come clean about many of my philanthropic activities from the past several decades. I'm not doing this to brag, and I'm certainly not doing it because I want the attention. I'm doing it for one and only one reason: to encourage other people to join me in helping the less fortunate. If even one or two people read this and are inspired by my life story

to help others, then it'll be worth the awkwardness I feel
writing it all down.

Now, let's start this section with the thing that made the
most difference in my own life: supporting quality education.

## — FLYING WITH HAWKS —

ducation is hands down the best way to break the
poverty cycle and give people the skills and self-
respect they need to find success. I'm living proof.
But, as the old saying goes, you can't just give people fish.
That's just a short-term quick fix. Instead, you need to teach
them how to fish. That's how they learn how to solve the
problem for themselves for the rest of their lives. Education
teaches people how to fish and gives them the support they
need to break free of dependency and destitution. It's their
ticket to a better life.

I was all too familiar with the benefits of education
as an avenue of escape. After all, I credit my own
education—and, of course, the people who guided me—as
the single most important factor in my ascent from poverty
to success. Without the encouragement of my HAWKs,
Moses Johnson, and my instructors at Howard and the GM
Minority Dealer's Academy, I never would have achieved
what I did as a car dealer.

I genuinely believe anyone can change the whole
trajectory of his life by simply taking advantage of the

educational opportunities around him. Most of the people I grew up with never made it out of the Black Box like I did. The sad thing is, though, almost any of them *could* have. Nobody handed me anything special when I was a child. I had the same opportunities as anyone else. That's what frustrates me so much when I see someone ignoring such a guaranteed path to self-improvement. I saw this in my own family. You'll remember that I have a twin brother. He and I were born at the same time into the same family. We lived in the same house, faced the same terrible abuse and abandonment from our mother, went through the same seventeen moves as kids, dealt with the same constant hunger, and everything else. So, when people ask me what the biggest difference is between me and my twin brother, I always point to our contrasting commitments to education. While I was in my room studying, he was out goofing off. His grades weren't good, and he didn't do anything to stand out to his teachers. In high school, he moved to Miami with our mother while I chose to stay in Daytona to take advantage of the better school. He eventually dropped out to start working forty hours a week for an hourly wage. That's still where he is today, while I'm out living a very different life. I honestly believe it all comes down to education. He was just looking for a fish; I was looking for someone to teach

**Most of the people I grew up with never made it out of the Black Box like I did. The sad thing is, though, almost any of them *could* have.**

me *how* to fish. That, more than anything else, has made all the difference.

## — PAYING IT BACKWARD THROUGH EDUCATION —

I established the Tony March Foundation in 1994 as an outlet for paying it backward in my community. Because of my firm belief that education is the best way to overcome poverty, the sole focus of the foundation for its first several years was funding educational projects. What we were able to do for the students in the Hartford public school system are some of the most meaningful and rewarding accomplishments of my life. At that time, 60 percent of those students were minorities, mostly black and Hispanic kids, and they needed some help. I was honored to have the chance to lend them a hand up, but I never made it a *handout*. I made sure these students understood how important their education was, so I did my best to tie our support to their own hard work. Let me tell you about a few things we did with the foundation and some other things I've personally done with and for the students of Hartford over the years.

### Awarding the Greatest Challenge: Showing Up

You can have the best teachers and schools in the country, but if students are absent from class, they're not going

to receive a quality education. In the late '90s, I knew
Hartford's public schools had an especially hard time with
truancy; attendance was spotty, at best. It was the opposite
of my experience in school, where I only missed five days
of class from first grade through my high school graduation.
I wanted to be there even when I was sick because I knew
something a lot of students never figure out: If you're in
class, you have a chance to learn something. If you're not in
class, you have no chance of learning anything. Hartford's
students needed that chance.

When your home life is unstable and
you don't have positive role models, it's hard to understand
the importance of simply showing up for school. I realized
some students need an incentive to attend class. Sure, it
would be nice if kids showed up just for the chance to learn,
but let's be honest: most elementary and high school students
aren't that future-focused. So, I proposed a tangible reward
that could make a major difference in their lives and reverse
school truancy at the same time. The idea I came up with

was so crazy that it received a lot of national media coverage. And, best of all, it worked.

I told the school superintendent I wanted to give away either a new car or $10,000 cash to a student who had perfect school attendance during the academic year. If more than one student qualified, I suggested drawing names to determine the winner. The superintendent accepted my offer—how could he not—and announced the details of the perfect attendance award to students at the start of the school year.

The results were unbelievable. In the first year of the program, perfect attendance increased by *70 percent*! We kept it up year after year, and things began to snowball. We kept adding more prizes through new companies and sponsors who wanted to get involved. Before long, students had the chance to win cars, cash, trips to Walt Disney World, computers, and thousands of dollars' worth of other prizes. This was huge for the children, because most of them came from homes that could never afford such luxuries. Eventually, there were so many prizes that it took hours to distribute them all and large crowds came to enjoy the show. It looked like a county fair with clowns, cotton candy, balloons, attractions, and thousands of people celebrating the hardworking students.

**Before long, students had the chance to win cars, cash, trips to Walt Disney World, computers, and thousands of dollars' worth of other prizes.**

The car (or cash equivalent) was always the most coveted prize of the day. The name of each child with perfect attendance was placed on a piece of paper and put in a hopper, and a local celebrity drew the winning name. We required students to be present to win—this was an attendance award, after all—and were always surprised when the winning child wasn't there. This happened three different years! After having a year of perfect attendance, the student didn't show up to get the car.

Of course, everyone in the crowd was thrilled when that happened, because it gave all the other contestants a second shot at the prize. One of our winners ended up in *People* magazine. This one was probably my favorite experience in all the years we gave cars and cash away because it perfectly captures why we did it. The winner was a first-grader whose mother didn't even drive. The family was terribly poor, though, and needed the $10,000 more than anything. I can still picture the desperation and determination on that mother's face. Despite such bad circumstances, that little girl still showed up for school every single day. Maybe she did it hoping to win the money for her family; maybe she did it just because she wanted to be a good student. Either way, can you imagine the mother's face when we called that girl's name? She broke down crying and the whole family covered us up in hugs as we handed them the $10,000. They couldn't believe it. To them, it was like winning $1 million. I still get a little choked up thinking about it.

The perfect attendance award program became so successful that it spun off a related program called the

Hartford Public School First Day Program. Think of it like a one-day perfect attendance award. The superintendent came up with the idea because the schools had a terrible time getting inner-city kids to class for the first day of school each year. And, since you couldn't win the yearlong perfect attendance award without being there the very first day of the school year, it made sense to tie the two together. Local businesses stepped up again with prizes for the first day program, and they were given out in the auditorium on the opening day. The prizes obviously weren't as big as the end-of-the-year awards celebration, but they still meant a lot to the children who won.

Some may argue that offering these prizes is just a way to bribe kids into going to class. I think I'm okay with that. Children can't always see the long-term good of going to school, so I'm all for anything that will get them through the doors and into their seats. Hopefully, once they're in class, they'll catch a passion for learning and want to keep coming back for the right reasons. But, if a new backpack, a new pair of shoes, or even the hope of winning a car can get them to their desks in front of a dedicated teacher, I'd do that all day long.

## Dream in Detail

While every student can and will benefit from taking education seriously, I always love targeting middle school students—seventh and eighth graders—with a special motivational talk I call Dream in Detail. Kids at that age are old enough to understand the message, but they're still young enough to put it into action to improve their chances of success in school. So, I made the message inspirational and practical, something they'd *want* to do and something they *could* do. It is a one-hour address geared to make the students believe they can succeed even under the most trying circumstances (poverty, broken homes, lack of encouragement, etc.) while providing them with a practical tool—my Dream in Detail chart—they can use to map out short- and long-term plans to achieve their dreams.

Every time I give this talk, I approach it with four key goals in mind:

1. **Provide a positive role model for children.** Too often, particularly in impoverished neighborhoods, kids are looking up to the pimps and drug dealers. And why not? They have the money, the fast cars, and the swagger. It's important to me to show kids that there are other ways to be successful.

2. **Give children hope for their future.** I use the old "If I can make it, anyone can make it" approach using my story. I tell them how I grew up, what I overcame, and how I still got a good education and became a successful businessman. And then I try to make them believe they can do it too.

**3. Teach the importance of planning ahead.** I teach kids how to set goals and use those goals to achieve anything they want in life.

**4. Emphasize the importance of staying in school.** I stress how education is the best tool for overcoming a life of poverty and enhancing one's chances for self-sufficiency, financial success, and personal satisfaction.

I've given this message to hundreds of middle school classes, and I plan to keep giving it as often as I can for the rest of my life. I wish there was a way to know for sure how effective it is at keeping kids in school. All I really have to go by is the engagement I see in the students' eyes and their posture while I'm talking. Also, I guess I can assume it's making a difference based on how often teachers ask me to come back year after year to address their classes. My big takeaway, I think, is that children are thirsty for success stories. They desperately want to see firsthand how people just like them overcame seemingly impossible circumstances and made something of themselves.

I usually start by having the classroom teacher introduce me, giving just enough detail to establish my credibility and pique the students' interest. The teacher will drop in a few things that kids find especially impressive, like the fact that I own several car dealerships, some sports teams, and almost purchased the New England Patriots. This gets them ready to listen, but then I still have to win them over myself. I know I always have to establish my own credibility in the first minute or two of a presentation, so I tell the kids I'm the CEO of a very large company. I follow that up by asking if anybody knows how many zeros are in $100 million. A student occasionally takes a guess, but usually there are no replies. So, I write the number on the board, taking my time as I slowly write each zero. Once they seem impressed enough by that figure, I tell them my company has sales worth more than that. That's usually enough to earn me a few precious minutes of a seventh-grader's attention.

While they're looking at the board, taking in the fact that a multimillionaire is standing in their classroom, I always hit them with the clincher: "I went from where you are right now to running a successful business with that many zeros in sales. And I'm here to tell you how you can do it too."

I've done this long enough to know that some students still won't believe I'm *really* one of them, so I play a little game with them. I tell everyone to put their hand up and keep it up while I ask a series of questions. I say, "Only put your hand down when you have to answer *no* to one of these questions." I start with something easy, such as "Do you have at least one parent living with you at home?" and "Have you ever had to move into a different home?" Usually, most hands are still in the air. Then, I ask,

"Have you moved two times in your life? Three times in your life? Four times?" This is usually when hands start dropping. Next, I say, "You're in the seventh grade, right? How many of you have already moved eight times since you were in first grade?" At this point there are usually no hands in the air. If there are one or two, I'll ask, "Have you ever lived in an orphanage?" I've never had any hands left in the air by this point.

Looking over the mostly quiet classroom, I say, "I was raised in the projects. By the time I was your age, I'd already moved fifteen times. I also lived in an orphanage for a while. So, even though I own a large company now, I didn't start off as some rich guy. I lived in poverty. My family had less money in a week than some of you have in your pockets right now. Sometimes, I ate food out of garbage cans to survive. I lived with twelve people in a 900-square-foot house, and I didn't own a single new piece of clothing until I was in the eleventh grade."

Once the kids are convinced that I'm legit, I hand out my Dream in Detail chart, the same chart I used myself to go from poverty to victory. Then, I say, "A dream without a plan is just a dream. I can't guarantee that every one of you who uses this chart will become as successful as me. But I can guarantee that, if you use it, you'll have a better chance of becoming successful."

## — DREAM IN DETAIL CHART —

he chart is pretty simple. It gives students space to write goals in three different categories: career, education, and social life. Then, they can write down where they want to be in each area in one, three, five, and ten years.

|  | 1 YEAR | 3 YEARS | 5 YEARS | 10 YEARS |
|---|---|---|---|---|
| **CAREER** |  |  |  |  |
| **EDUCATION** |  |  |  |  |
| **SOCIAL LIFE** |  |  |  |  |

I explain to them the difference between a dream, a goal, and a plan. I say, "You start with a dream. But, when you write that dream down on paper and put a deadline on it, it becomes a goal. Then, when you break that goal down into steps, it becomes a plan. Then, when you back up that plan with action, it becomes a reality. That's what I want to happen for you. I want to show you how to turn your dreams into goals, your goals into a plan, and your plan into reality."

With the chart in their hands, I ask the students to consider what they want to be in life. They probably won't know exactly what they want to do with their lives, but it's important for them to at least start thinking about how their strengths and interests might line up with certain careers. I use my own career choice as an example. "If you want to be an engineer, that dream has a specific path that includes high school math, physics, and chemistry. I was fortunate in that I knew at your age that I wanted to be an engineer, so I was able to start taking the appropriate math classes at just the right time. It's a lot harder to decide in eleventh or twelfth grade that you want to be an engineer (and hope to have a reasonable chance of making it) because engineering schools look at the math and science courses you took in high school. That means you have to start taking the appropriate courses as early as your freshman year. These kinds of classes build on each other, so you have to take them in the right sequence, like going from algebra to geometry to trigonometry. If you don't start the sequence early enough, you won't be able to finish before graduation."

**This may seem overly basic to some people, but remember, most of these kids don't have good role models.**

This may seem overly basic to some people, but remember, most of these kids don't have good role models. They don't have any successful people to look up to and emulate. I don't want to dumb it down too much for them, but I also don't want to take anything for granted. Based on the success I've had with this presentation over the years, I think you'd be surprised how many kids would miss this basic lesson if someone didn't take them by the hand and walk them through it.

With the help of their teacher, I have the students fill in the education section of the chart, followed by the social life and career sections. I want them looking ahead to the future and visualizing what their lives might look like. What do they want to do with their lives? What kind of people should they spend their time with? How will their friends and relationships impact the goals they've set for themselves? I want them to put it all on the chart, even though they won't be totally sure of their future plans at this age. The whole point is to get them dreaming about their futures and turning those dreams into goals they can work toward. Then, as they grow older and get a better sense of who they are and where they want to go, they can update the chart to make sure it always reflects their current set of goals.

This little goal chart has kept me moving forward for nearly sixty years. I know if I can get students used to it before they hit high school, the sky will be the limit for them.

## Adopting a Classroom

As I spent more time in classrooms, I realized the effectiveness of my presentation relied heavily on the involvement of an energetic, committed teacher. That's exactly the kind of teacher I found in the eighth-grade classroom at Burns Middle School. She greeted me warmly and spoke with genuine enthusiasm when she told the class about the speech that was in store for them. Their response was great. The students listened to my every word, and they bombarded me with questions after my presentation. This class really seemed to *get it*. They grabbed onto the idea that, despite any odds and obstacles, they could achieve high levels of success for themselves. Everyone in the class even hand wrote individual thank-you cards for me. That's when I *really* knew they had a wonderful teacher.

At the end of my first presentation to the eighth graders at Burns Middle School, the teacher put me on the spot, saying in front of the class, "You *are* coming back, aren't you, Mr. March?" How could I say no? Two months later, I kept that promise and returned. As I watched that teacher interact with her students, I could tell she was devoted to each and every child. She reminded me so much of my HAWK teachers who changed my life with their care and attention. It wasn't long before I offered to help by buying supplies for her classroom and even offering up small cash incentives, like a $100 prize for the winner of an essay contest. She accepted my help on one condition: that I return to deliver my Dream in Detail presentation every year to each of her new classes.

I basically adopted that class of eighth graders every year, making sure they had what they needed and stopping by throughout the year to engage with the students. The teacher caught some heat from the other teachers for this; they wanted me to help them with *their* classes too. The principal, however, was happy with how things were going. He told the other teachers, "If you want what this class has, you should go out and find your own Tony March." I'm happy to say that many of them did, giving other leaders in the community a chance to get involved.

Sometime later, I got a call from General Motors, asking if I could help them with a new marketing campaign. They were developing a series of television commercials that didn't necessarily promote its cars, but rather highlighted good things GM was doing in the community. I mentioned to them that I had recently adopted an eighth-grade class, and the marketing guy nearly burst with excitement. He said, "That's perfect! Kids and animals are guaranteed winners with these TV spots! Let's tape you in the class giving a speech to the kids. It'll have great audience appeal."

It took nine weeks of planning between the teacher, the principal, and the television people to get schedules coordinated and the details locked down. The day of filming, the crew had blocked off one entire wing of the school. Something as simple as a quick shot of the students running down the hallway took hours to film because they had to build a track for the camera to roll down. The same thing happened outside, when they had to shut down an entire street in front of the school to film students getting on the bus. Everything took longer and was ten times more complicated than I ever would have imagined. It made me glad I had gone into the car business instead of the entertainment industry!

The children, however, were captivated the entire time. They were thrilled when they found out they'd be on national television. These were inner-city kids; the only time they ever got media exposure was when something bad happened in their neighborhood. But here was a professional film crew who'd come to their school to meet then and turn them into stars. Besides getting bragging rights about being on TV, the students also got a glimpse into what all goes on behind the scenes to bring something to life on television. They were able to see all the preparation that went into the shoot and were allowed to approach the director and camera crew to ask questions. The children ate it up. None of the kids was paid to appear in the commercial, and they all had to come to school an hour early the day of filming. Still, every parent signed a release form and every child was present and accounted for that day. It was a big deal for them—and for me.

When the kids arrived at school, they were brought into a classroom where the wardrobe department had set up one hundred brand-new outfits. The students were told to pick out an outfit to wear for the commercial. Wearing a set of nice, new clothes for the day was exciting enough for these kids, but it got even better. The producers told the children that they could *keep* whatever outfit they picked out. Of all the things that happened that day, seeing the joy on their faces when they could keep their new outfits was by far my favorite moment. I knew exactly how these inner-city kids felt in that moment. It's something you just can't fully understand unless you've lived it. And I had certainly lived it.

It took sixteen hours over two days to create that thirty-second commercial—and only two of those sixteen hours were spent actually filming it. Those were a hard two hours, though. Many times, the students had to do as many as twenty takes of a single scene to get it just right. Lucky for us, their teacher knew how to keep them focused and well-behaved, even when things got a little frustrating. They learned a valuable lesson that day about patience and hard work. It gave them new insight into how much planning, time, and effort goes into something as deceptively simple as a short TV commercial.

At the end of the second day, I walked outside with the students to say goodbye. I couldn't get over the looks on their faces. They were beaming. For two magical days, all the hardships those kids faced on a daily basis were gone. They were excited, their spirits were light, and they were calling out, "Thank you! Thank you!" as they disappeared onto the school bus. It doesn't get any better than that.

The commercial aired nationally several months later, and my adopted class at Burns Middle School lit up television sets all across America several times a day. Whenever I saw it come up on the screen, I stopped whatever I was doing to watch it start to finish ... with a huge smile on my face.

## Building Future Business Leaders

As much as I've always loved working with middle school students, I knew high schoolers needed extra resources and opportunities too. Specifically, I felt a strong desire to help raise up a new generation of business leaders in predominately minority and inner-city schools. To that end, in 1986—years before I started the Tony March Foundation and refined my work in education—I worked with another local black businessman and the University of Connecticut to establish the Teenage Minority Business Program. This new program was designed to encourage Connecticut high school juniors and seniors who were black, Asian, Native American, and Hispanic to go to college, major in business, and become entrepreneurs.

All the participants were self-starters, which was important. Local principals told their students about the program at the beginning of the year, but then it was up to the students themselves to follow up and express their interest. The principals chose the best-suited participants from those who asked to be considered, and that elite group of students was invited to attend the program's three-day workshop at no cost.

During those three days, about seventy students lived on the University of Connecticut campus and learned about business from successful minority business owners, such as an owner of a fast-food franchise or a car dealership. For these students, interacting with minority entrepreneurs was not only educational but transformational. They saw undeniable proof that anyone, no matter where they came from or what color their skin was, could win in the business world. It gave them successful role models—something that is painfully lacking in many inner-city communities.

**I was talking mostly to kids who had no intention of going to college, and it was my job to convince them to at least consider it. For many, though, it remained a ridiculous idea.**

While I loved talking to middle school students, there was something extra special about speaking at the Teenage Minority Business Program. Any other time I spoke to students, I was talking mostly to kids who had no intention of going to college, and it was my job to convince them to at least consider it. For many, though, it remained a ridiculous idea. However, the students in the University of Connecticut program were a defined group of kids who already had dreams of attending college. It was an entirely different dynamic, and it gave me all-new opportunities to sell them the dream of future business success.

The Teenage Minority Business Program was such a hit that many other colleges and universities around the country developed their own versions of the retreat. While I loved seeing the idea spread and was proud to work with the University of Connecticut to provide this free educational opportunity to these students, the biggest win for me came years later when I heard back from several of these students. Many of our program alumni ultimately graduated high school, studied business in college, and went on to launch

new businesses of their own. Looking back, I can point
to dozens of minority-owned businesses that were at least
partially influenced by our retreat. There aren't many things
in my life that give me more satisfaction than that.

## — A TERRIBLE THING TO WASTE —

f anyone understood the importance of college financial
support, it was me. I don't know where I'd be without the
financial assistance and scholarships I received for Howard
University, but I know for a fact my life would be entirely
different today. Truthfully, that alternate reality is so painful
to consider that I can feel my anxiety rise when I think about
young people who have big college ambitions and little to no
means. That's the reason why the United Negro College
Fund (UNCF) has been such a big focus for me
for more than forty years.

Back in the 1970s, while working as an
engineer at General Motors, I made regular
contributions to the UNCF. Of course, the checks were
small back then, but I did what I could to support a cause I
truly believed in. The UNCF had annual televised telethons
that were hosted by Lou Rawls for twenty-five years. I
remember watching that telethon for hours every year as Lou
introduced other big-name black entertainers to perform in
what he famously called *Lou Rawls Parade of Stars*. It was a
great show and an even better cause.

In 1985, the year I opened my first car dealership,
I wanted to take my UNCF sponsorship to the next level.
Rather than simply sitting at home and watching the telethon,
I contacted the local UNCF chapter and asked how I could
help with that year's fundraiser. I threw myself into all facets of
the telethon, from lining up the volunteers to work the phones
to finding donors to pledge their support before the show was
on the air. I was surprised to learn that the organizers wanted
a large amount of money, around 80 percent of their goal,
already committed *before* the show goes live on TV. This gets
people excited, and it ensures the telethon will have a positive
outcome. I did my part by approaching my own business
contacts and getting about $500,000 in pledges from my own
personal network.

My involvement grew bit by bit over the next few
years. In 1988, the members of the GM Minority Dealer
Association, of which I was president, voted to give 100
percent of its charitable contributions to the UNCF. It
was a huge investment, and we were honored when they
announced our donation on air during the telethon. Apart
from the association, I donated $100,000 and every dealership
I owned contributed $6,000 every year. As the number of
dealerships grew, so did our UNCF contributions. I was
blown away when that number topped six figures, but that's
the kind of thing that happens with scale. In 1987 and 1989,
the UNCF gave me its Meritorious Service Award for my
fundraising efforts. The award was nice, of course, but
my real joy came in knowing how many young, minority

college students were getting the chance to change their lives through education with the money I helped UNCF collect. I hoped no other college freshman would have to survive an entire semester on a single fifty-cent, vending-machine hot dog a day like I did.

Always a fan of the telethon, I served as state chairman for the UNCF telethon from 1991 to 2003. Every year I, was inspired to hit a bigger number, and we raised millions of dollars during that time. In 1995, I received the UNCF's Distinguished Service Award for sponsoring the local UNCF telecast, which ran in conjunction with the national Lou Rawls telethon.

I'm not as active and hands-on these days, but I still support the UNCF and will until the day I die. If someone has the motivation to attend college and make a mark on this world, money should not stand in the way. It seems like yesterday when I was there myself, believing in my heart that education would allow me to rewrite my story.

## — A COMMITMENT TO HIGHER EDUCATION —

This chapter has detailed a few of the things I did in service to education over the years. While I spend most of my time serving K–12 students, I still dipped my toes into the college waters at times. I was happy to spend some time in an advisory role at Hartford Seminary and the University of Hartford, where I was appointed to the board of regents. This position gave me an inside look at the inner financial workings of colleges and universities. I was honestly surprised by what I found, including how much parents are willing to pay to send their children to a private college. I was also taken with how much the university spent on security. Clearly, parents who spend that much on their children's education want to know they will be safe. It was also nice to see that some schools, especially private schools, offer smaller class sizes. This enhances the learning process and promotes more student–teacher interaction.

All these academic luxuries came at a price, however. I soon learned the university president's top priority was raising funds. I always pictured him walking around with his arms outstretched, hoping cash would fall from the sky. I swear, only one hour of that man's day was spent on academic matters and the rest was on soliciting funds. It seemed like a strange way for a university's top officer to spend his time.

Even while I was serving in a volunteer role at the university, my heart was still with younger students. In 2003, I gave the school system a $125,000 grant to build a medical clinic at one of its largest public schools, Weaver High School. This gave students consistent, comprehensive care without them having to miss class. The clinic also had a public entrance that allowed it to serve the community outside of school hours. A year after it was built, I was blown away when I learned the school board voted to name it the Tony March

Adolescent Clinic. It's hard to find the words to say how much that meant to me. I only got medical treatment twice all throughout my school years; to think of all the students who'd have access to quality care right there at the school brought tears to my eyes. The whole thing was made even sweeter when the school board awarded me the Hartford Public School's Award of Distinction.

**A year after it was built, I was blown away when I learned the school board voted to name it the Tony March Adolescent Clinic.**

When I was young, pushing open the school doors revealed a world of safety and possibility to me. I was so grateful to be able to create that same feeling for other children. If I am ever only remembered for one thing, I hope it's for my commitment to helping all children—especially poor, inner-city, minority kids like I was—get a quality education.

I'll say it again: education is the most powerful tool we have to pull young men and women out of poverty. Whether you have students in the fight or not, I know you can make a difference. Get involved in your community. Talk to the teachers in your area. Find out what they need and how you can help. Maybe you can adopt a class. Maybe you can provide supplies or scholarships to class field trips. Better yet, maybe you can give money *and* time by finding ways to mentor these boys and girls. Kids today need positive role models just as badly as I did way back when. You never know what the students you help will go on to do with their lives. And trust me, dreaming of that is by far the greatest personal benefit I've ever had by helping students.

I hope you'll find out for yourself someday how that feels.

# SEVEN

# Serving a Few, Serving Many, and Serving Myself

"We think sometimes that poverty is only being hungry, naked, and homeless. The poverty of being unwanted, unloved, and uncared for is the greatest poverty. We must start in our own homes to remedy this kind of poverty."

~ MOTHER TERESA ~

You can't spend a quarter-century living, working, raising a family, and serving somewhere without growing to love it. That was me in Hartford. I had never planned on moving to Connecticut; I'd always imagined spending most of my career in Detroit. However, from the moment I moved to Hartford in 1985, I felt a special connection to the city. Since my first dealership there was in a declining area—and especially since my first apartment there was in a *terrible* area—I learned pretty quickly that Hartford, Detroit, and Daytona Beach weren't all that different. I guess every city in the country has some really nice parts of town and some really shady parts of town. In Hartford, I was fortunate to live and work in both.

During the twenty-five years I lived there, I was able to get involved in many different service opportunities of all different sizes. I've learned that there's never a cookie-cutter, one-size-fits-all way to help other people. Sometimes, helping Hartford meant serving dinner to a homeless person in a shelter and sitting down to share a cup of coffee with him afterward. I've done that ... *a lot*. Sometimes, though, the responsibilities were a lot bigger and, honestly, more intimidating—like the years I was entrusted to figure out the best way to spend more than $1 billion in unexpected state assistance money. That one was crazy, but the heart of service is always the same, whether your opportunity seems small or whether it seems bigger than you can handle. Whatever you're doing, whatever the opportunity is, the goal of service is to simply help as many people as you can with however much time and money you can spare. Let me show you what I mean by telling you about some of the big and small ways I was able to help serve the people of Hartford.

## — HELPING THE HOMELESS —

've often said that I was *blessed* to have moved seventeen times before graduating high school—and that includes the three-month stay at the orphanage. Why do I call this a blessing? It's because the constant state of moving around and complete lack of permanence have enabled me to understand the plight of the homeless on a personal level. I know how it feels to live out of grocery bags and eat out of garbage cans. I remember going to bed one night and wondering where I'd sleep the next. It's a special kind of insecurity—a total *lack* of security—that you can only understand if you've lived it. No amount of success in the car industry could ever wipe away those painful memories. I'm glad for that, because that's what's fueled my passion for helping the homeless all these years. Of all the different ways I've been able to help other people, there's still nothing quite like getting my hands dirty and serving others with the bare essentials: food and shelter. That's what I was able to do at Hartford's Mercy homeless shelter.

> **I remember going to bed one night and wondering where I'd sleep the next. It's a special kind of insecurity—a total *lack* of security.**

## Loving People with Mercy

I started volunteering at Mercy in 1985. I did whatever they needed me to do, but my passion was working in the kitchen. I made meals, unpacked boxes, cleaned dishes, mopped floors, and did all sorts of a less-than-glamorous kitchen tasks. It didn't matter to me; working in the kitchen meant I was helping to feed hungry people. That's something that's been important to me ever since I escaped the Black Box. If I could help just one person avoid garbage-cake tapeworms, I knew it was all worth it.

The fact that I was there during the week and not just on holidays got the attention of the shelter's director, Paul

Laffin. Paul used to say, "People do their volunteering once
or twice a year, like going to church on Christmas and
Easter. But homeless people are hungry 365 days a year."
The first time I heard him say that, I became a regular
volunteer, because I knew they needed consistent help.
Being around the shelter more meant being around Paul
more, and that was just fine with me. He was a huge man
who laughed a lot and filled every conversation with details
about his work with the homeless, his love of baseball, or
both. He was like a big teddy bear, with a heart as big as
Jesus's and a Red Sox ball cap forever perched on his giant
head. Paul was the voice of the homeless in Hartford, and he
lived and breathed his cause. All his love and affection went
to the people at the shelter.

Paul and I became good friends. More than that, he
became my mentor, teaching me all the ins and outs of running
a homeless shelter. Within just a few months, Paul asked me
to help supervise the volunteers. Soon, he was walking me
through all the everyday procedures, like screening potential
residents and the best practices for providing food, clothing,
and a safe environment during their stay. He even showed
me how to run a successful discharge when someone left the
shelter, much like a hotel manager helps a guest check out. Paul
also knew I liked to work the grill in the kitchen, so he made
sure to bring me back there whenever pancakes or burgers was
on the menu.

Paul and I spent a lot of time together. We were kindred
spirits, and it wasn't long before we were treating each other

like family. We'd pick each other's brains when searching for solutions to problems. If the shelter's van broke down, I'd get my used car manager to find a good replacement to give to the shelter. That was the kind of relationship we developed. I talked about Paul and Mercy shelter so often that my employees started getting involved too. Knowing how important the shelter was to me, they stopped giving me Christmas gifts directly and instead made cash gifts to Mercy in my name. No other gift could have made me happier. Or, if we knew a specific need, my employees and I would go in together to buy whatever the shelter needed that year. I loved seeing how my employees started finding ways to help Mercy; sometimes, I wasn't even involved in what they did!

## The Gospel According to Paul

Paul had strong opinions about the best way to serve homeless people, and, to be honest, a few of his opinions went against my gut instincts. For example, when a homeless person approached me, I was always happy to give him a few dollars. Paul always beat me up over this, telling me I wasn't *really* helping them and was actually doing them a disservice. He was firm in his conviction that people should *never* give money to panhandlers on the street. He argued they'd use the cash to buy cigarettes, alcohol, or drugs. He'd say giving them cash was the quickest way to feed their bad habits, thereby guaranteeing they'd stay on the streets instead of getting help. He felt so strongly about it that he didn't allow people to take food packages outside the shelter, for fear they would sell them for drug money on the streets.

I have to admit that Paul was probably right about that one. I'll never forget driving to the shelter one day and seeing a homeless person standing on a street corner holding a sign that read, "Can you spare some money to feed the homeless?" I had a hunch about this guy, so I rolled down the window and said, "I'm sorry, I can't give you any money. What you need to do is go to the homeless shelter. They can help you. They have plenty of food to eat and a safe, warm place to sleep."

The guy shook his head. "Nah, I just need some money," he said, pointing to his sign.

Following Paul's advice, I stood my ground and said, "I'm sorry, I won't give you money. But I'm going to the homeless shelter right now, and I think you should too." The man shook his head again, said something under his breath, and shuffled away from my car. He wanted to try his luck with car behind me before the light changed.

You know how real estate agents are always going on and on about "location, location, location"? Well, that's true with panhandling too. You see, this guy who *needed* some cash was posted right in front of a giant liquor store. It didn't take much imagination for me or anyone else to picture what he'd do the instant someone handed him a $20 bill. It's a trap I might have fallen for if I didn't have Paul's voice screaming in my ear every time I saw someone asking for money.

As firm as he was about never giving panhandlers cash, Paul's strongest warning was about never letting a homeless person in your car. He always told the volunteers at Mercy, "Never *ever* allow a panhandler or homeless person in your car. You are courting danger when you do this, and it *will not end well.*"

Over time, the wisdom of Paul's warning about handing out cash sunk in, and I stopped giving money to panhandlers. I still wanted to help them, though, and I certainly wasn't going to stop talking to them, so I changed tactics. Whenever I was stopped at a stoplight and someone knocked on my window asking for money, I'd ask, "I don't have any cash to give you, but would you like to earn some money today?" If they were interested, I'd say, "Jump in, and I'll take you to my dealership. You can wash some cars and make a day's wages." It was a surefire way to figure out who wanted drug money and who wanted real help.

When a panhandler took me up on my offer, I dropped them off with my service manager, who would immediately put the person to work cleaning cars. I'm happy to report that more than one hundred people accepted that offer over the years. This let me build a relationship with several homeless people around town because I always remembered the ones who chose to work for the day. It made me feel better about giving them a few bucks if I saw them on the street later.

When Paul found out about my little "let me drive you to work at my car dealership" offer, he just about lost his mind. He argued that I wasn't just putting myself in danger by letting them in my car, but that I was actually inviting danger by telling them I was a successful business owner. He railed on this for several years before I finally gave in and found another way to help panhandlers work for some money. In hindsight, I know Paul was right about the dangers of letting strangers in your car. I did it more than a hundred times, though, and nothing bad ever happened to me. Maybe it was God taking care of me while I tried to take care of people, or maybe I just got lucky. Either way, it's not something I'd ever recommend someone else try.

I worked with Mercy shelter regularly for more than twenty years. During my time volunteering there, I went from a rookie owner of a single car dealership to a multimillionaire with more than twenty-one dealerships. My life changed a lot over those decades, but one thing never did: my commitment to serve the homeless people of Hartford. It was such a simple, easy thing for me to do—for *anyone* to do—but it makes such a big difference to the shelters who work tirelessly 365 days a year to meet the needs of society's homeless and hungry.

## — A $1 BILLION OPPORTUNITY —

I loved my time serving at Mercy shelter. It gave me the chance to get to know hurting people on a personal level. I got to sit with them, hear their stories, and find ways to meet their specific needs one-on-one. That's how I always envisioned my service to others. I never wanted to be a nameless, faceless benefactor who hid away in a far-off office simply writing checks. Instead, I loved the hands-on, nitty-gritty, sometimes-dirty opportunities Mercy provided. However, you can only go so far helping people one at a time. While I loved the personal contact the shelter provided, I also tried to keep my eye on the bigger picture and find ways to serve the whole city full of hurting people. Even I was surprised, though, when a $1 billion opportunity literally fell into my lap that brought my two specialties—enterprise and philanthropy—together in a wild and unique way. And it all started with a football team.

### Stadium Scandal

The New England Patriots is one of the most successful sports franchises in the world. They've played in the Super Bowl a record eleven times, and Tom Brady holds the quarterback record with six wins under his belt. With eighteen consecutive winning seasons at the time of this writing, they're close to breaking the league's record for consecutive winning seasons, currently held by the Dallas Cowboys at twenty seasons. To put it mildly, the Pats are a big deal in New England.

They've had their share of controversy too. Who could forget "Deflategate," when Brady was accused of throwing underinflated footballs against the Indianapolis Colts in 2015? Or "Spygate" in 2007, when they were caught videotaping coaching signals of the New York Jets from an unauthorized position on the field? Long before any of these scandals, though, there was "Stadiumgate," a failed attempt to move the team that had a lasting, profound effect on the city of Hartford. And, somehow, I was at the center of it.

Hartford has a complicated relationship with the Patriots. In fact, in the early nineties, I was part of a group of investors who came close to buying the team and moving it to Connecticut. It was exciting for me to see all the financial data on how an NFL team is set up, all the TV and sponsor contracts, and all the financial information on the league. That deal fell apart, and Patriots owner James Orthwein later sold the team in 1994 to Robert Kraft, a savvy Massachusetts businessman with interests in manufacturing, media, and sports. He'd been a loyal Pats fan for decades, and owning the team was a lifelong dream come true for him. He shared Orthwein's longtime frustration about the team, though, which was the outdated, run-down home stadium in Boston. Orthwein had thought about moving the team out of Boston for the past couple of years, and now Kraft was publicly considering it as well. Despite his pleas for renovations, the Massachusetts legislature didn't seem interested in raising funds for a new stadium. So, Kraft began to look elsewhere.

When the news broke that the Patriots were open to moving out of Massachusetts, the Connecticut legislature sprang into action. With a "build it and they will come" philosophy, the state took a gamble and approved a $1 billion funding package that included a state-of-the-art stadium.

In November 1998, Connecticut Governor John Rowland made the Patriots' move from Boston to Hartford sound like a done deal. "This is an historic day for the Hartford community," he said at a press conference. "It's a turning point that will propel this city and the state into the next century. I'm here to sign a memo of understanding with Robert Kraft. It's the first step in a process that will conclude on December 31 of this year. If we are successful, as I'm sure we will be over the next forty-five days, the New England Patriots will play their first home game in Hartford in the fall of 2001."[1]

*The Hartford Courant* ran a "Patriots Extra Edition" the next day, with Rowland and Kraft smiling on the front page under the headline, "Touchdown! Deal Gives Hartford Home Field Advantage." The thought of moving a major NFL franchise to our city, knowing we'd already set aside $1 billion to give them the best possible home stadium, was a major win for Hartford. We were thrilled!

[1] Mike Reiss, "Would Patriots' Move to Hartford Have Been Similar to Chargers' Move to L.A.?" ESPN.com, October 26, 2017, http://www.espn.com/blog/new-england-patriots/post/_/id/4807311/would-patriots-move-to-hartford-have-been-similar-to-chargers-move-to-la.

Sadly, it was not to be. Robert Kraft pulled out of the deal five months later. He blamed his decision on construction delays, which didn't really make sense to those of us "in the know." But then, things became much clearer when the state of Massachusetts came up with $70 million to build a new stadium in Foxborough, near Boston, after decades of refusing funds.

The reaction in Hartford was understandable. We felt angry and used. State Tax Commissioner Kevin Sullivan, who was the leader in the Senate at the time, said, "Kraft played the State of Connecticut in order to leverage his position in Boston where he was always going to be. It was just a question of when they would write a bigger check and give him the benefits he wanted."[2]

Governor Rowland weighed in, saying, "No one walks away from a $374 million deal because a plan might be a year later than expected. And I suggested to [Kraft] that perhaps he had some other alternatives and plans in the works. I'm sure we'll find out more about that in the not-too-distant future."[3] State Senator Paul Doyle was even more blunt. He said we'd been fleeced and that the whole thing was a scam devised by Kraft to force Massachusetts into coughing up the money to build a new stadium. Having seen my share of shady business deals and shadier businesspeople, I tend to agree. Regardless, this whole mess left Hartford with no NFL team—and $1 billion in unexpectedly available funds. It was time for the city to shift gears.

[2] Mark Davis, "Was Robert Kraft Ever Sincere About Moving Patriots to Connecticut?" WTNH News 8, February 2, 2017, https://www.wtnh.com/news/connecticut/was-robert-kraft-ever-sincere-about-moving-patriots-to-connecticut_20180322100617551/1068447735.

[3] John Altavilla and Daniela Altimari, "Hartford Patriots? It Seemed Too Good To Be True," The Hartford Courant, February 4, 2017, https://www.courant.com/sports/football/hc-hartford-patriots-stadium-0205-20170204-story.html.

## What Do You Do with $1 Billion?

The Connecticut legislature faced a dilemma. It had created
an enormous urban renewal project and had raised enough
money to fund the entire $1 billion expenditure. The
centerpiece of the renewal was meant to be a state-of-the-art
NFL stadium that no one now needed or wanted. So, what
were they supposed to do? What else could Connecticut use
that money for and, just as important, who could be trusted
to oversee that much wealth?

A large portion of the $1 billion was originally earmarked
for redeveloping Hartford's inner city and helping its citizens
in a variety of social programs. I was excited to learn that
the state decided to double down on that investment by
budgeting the *entire* $1 billion for improving Hartford
and helping its poorest communities. To oversee this
unprecedented undertaking—the complete redevelopment
of downtown Hartford—the governor selected six respected
local leaders and appointed them to the new Capital City
Economic Development Authority (CCEDA). To my great
honor, I was asked to serve as one of its commissioners.

I didn't realize at the time how great a commitment this
would be. When all was said and done, I spent a full ten years
on the committee from 1998 to 2008, volunteering more
than a thousand hours a year working on CCEDA business.
In my opinion, losing the New England Patriots deal was
the best thing that could've happened to Hartford. A shiny
new stadium would have provided entertainment a few times
a year to the small percentage of people who could afford

NFL game tickets. Instead, we now had the means to make a life-changing difference for a large percentage of Hartford's citizens, many of whom lived well below the poverty level.

**When most people across the country hear Connecticut, they probably think of the Kennedys and yacht clubs, not homelessness and despair.**

I always saw Hartford as a textbook example of income disparity in America. Hartford was a small, dense city with a real poverty problem and a high minority rate of about 65 percent. It was also one of the poorest cities in the country. That's strange when you look at the context. The state of Connecticut has one of the highest incomes per capita in America. There is tremendous wealth all along the coast, it's the home of many Fortune 500 companies, and there are private schools everywhere. When most people across the country hear Connecticut, they probably think of the Kennedys and yacht clubs, not homelessness and despair. But Hartford had plenty of it.

So, as our commission settled into our work, we knew we were dealing with a circle of poverty completely enveloped by a ring of wealth. As commissioners of the CCEDA, we knew the kind of money the state had allocated to our project combined with a bold vision and realistic expectations gave us an unprecedented opportunity. We wanted to create the conditions to allow as many as possible to break loose from poverty and become contributing, self-sufficient members of society.

The CCEDA mandate was urban renewal. Our goal was to complete several projects that would revitalize downtown Hartford, including the construction of a new hotel, convention center, and parking garage, which would add nine thousand parking spaces in the downtown area. We were to revitalize the riverfront, demolish more than 450 vacant structures, and build and/or refurbish one thousand housing units for low-income families. Education was also a priority, as we were tasked with building a science center for the community and local schools—something I would have loved to have access to when I was a student working on my science fair project—as well as a community college. Finally, we were to set up the Hartford Construction Job Initiative, which would train local residents how to earn a decent wage performing key vocational skills.

### A Huge Leap for Hartford

These were huge goals, and I fully supported each one. However, I was most excited about the small handful of projects that promoted education and the ones that focused specifically on the people living in the projects. I saw these as *my people*; I knew how they lived, and I was excited about the chance to help them by getting involved in several key initiatives.

I helped organize the massive renovation of a six-story building in downtown Hartford to house an existing community college. The city wanted education that was accessible to all, but the school's location at the time was in an area that was difficult for students to reach, especially for those who didn't own a car. Its new home was on a major bus route, making it much easier to get to. The architects created a space that was comfortable and inviting, and it included technological upgrades to make it a truly modern facility. I appreciated the idea that we were giving a new lease on life to existing infrastructure, while doing the same for the students who could now attend the college.

While we were constructing some new buildings and renovating others, we were also charged with knocking many buildings down. We earmarked $55 million for the destruction of 450 abandoned structures in the downtown area. It was a daunting task. The bureaucracy involved in getting a teardown permit often took years, especially when absentee landlords were involved or property ownership was in question, which was typical. Multiply that time and trouble by 450, and you can imagine how much red tape it took to accomplish this goal.

But tearing down all those abandoned buildings served several important purposes. It eliminated condemned structures, getting homeless people and curious kids out of dangerous places. It removed hideaways where people gathered to do drugs and engage in other illegal activities. It reduced crime rates, decreased disease by eliminating breeding areas for rats and vermin, and removed eyesores from residential neighborhoods, which would, hopefully, increase property values.

Tearing hundreds of old buildings down is the kind of

project with hard-to-see benefits. There was no immediate economic value in the mass demolitions, but there was genuine value nonetheless. Removing condemned structures, dangerous buildings, and burnt-out eyesores made a significant difference in the quality of life for those in the area. Their communities started looking nice again, and that was a big win for us. Plus, the demolitions sent a message: the city of Hartford was stepping up its care for all its citizens.

One of our commission's most exciting ventures was creating home-ownership opportunities for poor, inner-city families. The CCEDA purchased two city blocks of two-story brownstone duplexes and completely renovated them. Then, families were selected to buy the properties at reasonable terms, move into the first floor, and rent out the second floor to tenants. This gave the new homeowners the chance to pay their mortgage payments using the rent money from their tenants. These were families who never could have afforded a home, but now, as long as they kept their rental units rented out, they were basically living in a house they owned for free while their tenants paid off their mortgages!

In a city full of substandard housing, people waited in

line to sign up for the chance to own one of these duplexes. The two streets we redeveloped were literally brand-new with new homes, sidewalks, and landscaping. Furthermore, we put safeguards in place for the residents' security. Potential residents had to sign a form agreeing that they could be evicted if caught using or even possessing drugs. Plus, each house was occupied by an actual homeowner, so there was a shared commitment to maintaining the area. It was a dream come true for families who wanted their kids to grow up in a stable, safe space.

One of my favorite projects, of course, was the science center. With my passion for engineering and my longtime love of science, you can imagine how excited I was to get personally involved with this $150-million venture. I had the opportunity to help with the design and construction of the building itself, and I also helped choose the permanent exhibits. The center was built to house ten major exhibits. Five of these were permanent fixtures in our science center, and five others would be touring exhibits that came from other museums. Construction began in January 2006, and the Connecticut Science Center opened to the public in June 2009.

## Teaching People How to Fish

I said earlier in this book that I've always preferred someone *teaching* me to fish instead of just *handing* me a fish. Long-term solutions, though not the easiest, are always better than a simple quick fix that still leaves you hungry and needy in the long run. That's why I was so excited about one particular part of the CCEDA's mandates. We weren't just building up and knocking down buildings; we were charged with building up *people* as well. To that end, the CCEDA was commissioned to ensure the creation of jobs and career opportunities for all of Hartford's residents, regardless of their education, income, or social status. To do it, we created the Hartford Construction Job Initiative (HCJI) in 1999. The HCJI was responsible for training disadvantaged and low-income Hartford residents with the skills and confidence to get (and keep) jobs in the construction industry, thereby giving them the tools to move from dependency to self-sufficiency. In short, we were teaching them to fish.

I was honored to chair that initiative. Give the poor an opportunity to participate in the revitalization of their hometown and improve their lot in life? Now you're talking my language.

The poor residents of Hartford had the odds stacked against them. Many didn't speak English, hadn't graduated from high school, didn't own cars, and were hardly proficient in math. Some were former drug users and former prison inmates. Others were single mothers on state assistance. But they all had dreams, and that's what we focused on. If they wanted to be a carpenter, iron worker, drywaller, mason—any trade, really—we would help make it happen.

We developed a vocational technical school, and, because we knew the pressures of everyday life were a factor, it included an impressive in-house day care center.

We refurbished the building so each floor could be dedicated to a specific trade. We had plumbers on one floor, electricians on the next, welding above that, and so on. When we were ready to launch, we invested in a big advertising campaign to let everyone—the public, private corporations, and most importantly, existing agencies who worked with the poor—know about this job training opportunity. We were open for business.

Here's how it worked: Case workers interviewed potential candidates to determine what (if any) interests and skills they had and then helped them figure out which vocation would suit them. From there, we provided whatever vocational training they needed to make it in their chosen field. We also made available other basic education opportunities, such as classes on English as a second language, GED prep, OSHA training, math, and more. We tried to make it a one-stop shop for anyone who sincerely wanted a shot at getting a good job and simply needed some help getting there.

The entire process worked like a funnel. Candidates were interviewed at the top and then passed through various training programs. By the time they came out the other end, they had the work competencies, trade certifications, and support necessary to find and hold construction and other trade jobs. A few years in, the "funnel" nickname became official. Since its inception in 1999, the Jobs Funnel has trained and placed more than 3,500 north-central Connecticut residents in well-paid, stable construction jobs.

The program helped the Hartford business community

as well. Before the Jobs Funnel, contractors were hard-pressed to find enough locals with the competency to work on a construction site. Because federal regulations required contractors to use a certain number of minority workers, they often had to hire from outside the city. So, the contractors were thrilled with what the HCJI was doing. We were helping them hit their quotas *and* providing some of the best-trained new employees they'd ever seen. It was a win–win–win!

After just a few years, it was clear the HCJI was a huge success. In fact, the Jobs Funnel received the National Association of Counties Workforce Development Award for Excellence in November 2002. The CCEDA job initiative model proved so successful that other cities modeled their own strategies after ours. It turns out imitation really is the highest form of flattery, and we were thrilled anytime another city copied what we were doing.

When Robert Kraft first floated the idea of moving the New England Patriots out of Boston, no one could have imagined what the long-term impact would be a hundred miles away in Hartford, Connecticut. I enjoy football as much as the next guy, and it would have been nice to have a major NFL team in my hometown all those years. But I would prefer to have the chance to spend $1 billion improving my city and the hard-working men and women who live there. I'd take the $1 billion in life-changing, community-shaping opportunities every time.

## — HEARTBREAK IN THE HOMELESS COMMUNITY —

n the late nineties, as I was trying to figure out how to serve Hartford with the $1 billion I'd been entrusted with through the CCEDA, I often thought of my friend Paul Laffin of Hartford's Mercy shelter. He always seemed to know what to do, and I greatly valued his friendship and advice. He never had the "worry" of managing $1 billion for the community, but I think he would have had some great ideas. Sadly, he wasn't around long enough to share them with me. Paul died unexpectedly in 1999, just one year into my commission with the CCEDA.

His death rocked our community and shook Mercy to its foundation. The entire civic community knew Paul by name and often referred to him as a saint long before his death. Sometimes, his heart seemed so big and his work so great that it was difficult for the rest of us to remember he was merely a man. He was, in fact, a *superman* who loved everyone and who was loved by everyone. And that's what made his death—and the way he died—so incomprehensible.

One afternoon, Paul was sitting on a bench on the shelter grounds, enjoying one his frequent, yet admittedly ill-advised, cigarette breaks. It was the same bench he and I shared countless times when we took a break together during a long, hard day of serving Hartford's homeless. On this fateful day, however, tragedy struck. As Paul relaxed on the bench, a shelter resident came up behind him and stabbed him to death. We learned in the course of the investigation that the perpetrator was mentally ill and had nothing personal against Paul at all. He would have killed anyone in his path that day; it just happened to be Paul. The crime was a senseless act of violence by a very disturbed and sick man—just the kind of person Paul always strove to help.

Paul's funeral was one of the biggest ever held in Hartford. His memorial service was held at St. Patrick–St. Anthony, the city's largest and most beautiful church. It was standing room only inside, with another large crowd of mourners gathered on the street. At the end of his service, the archbishop sang the Salve Regina prayer, something usually reserved for the death of a priest. They apparently made an exception for our own St. Paul, who was buried with his trademark Red Sox cap still perched on his head.

That day, as we all gathered to mourn our friend, someone commented, "Paul may be gone, but he'll never be forgotten." How true that is. I've certainly never forgotten him. In fact, to this day, I write "to the memory of Paul Laffin" on every check I write to Mercy's homeless shelter.

**To this day, I write "To the memory of Paul Laffin" on every check I write to Mercy's homeless shelter.**

The city of Hartford started writing his name on things too. One morning the spring after Paul's death, I was driving to my dealership at Exit 33 just off I-91. With my dealership in sight, I passed over the last bridge before my exit. I looked to my right and saw a new sign that said Paul Laffin Memorial Bridge. It took my breath away. I was touched that the city of Hartford loved Paul so much that it memorialized him with a highway marker. But how was it possible that, of all the streets in town, the one that led right to my dealership was named after my close friend? Was it really just a crazy coincidence, or was this another example of providence making itself known in my life? Regardless, I now had a daily reminder right in front of me of my mentor Paul and his tireless work for the homeless.

I stepped up my efforts at Paul's shelter, but, even with all of us working harder than before, it was impossible to fill the void he left. Still, I loved the work I was able to do there, and I guess the feeling was mutual. In 2003, the Mercy Homeless Housing Shelter gave me its Humanity Award for my financial help and volunteer work. I knew Paul was smiling down on me that day...and reminding me not to pick up stray panhandlers on the side of the road anymore.

It's now been twenty years since Paul's death, but I still tear up whenever I think of him. Even in death, though, Paul continues to mentor me. Whenever I'm faced with a decision on how to best help someone or meet a need, I think back to the long conversations Paul and I had on that bench and in the kitchen at Mercy. His voice is still there, echoing in my head and giving me good advice. Paul even gave me a picture of how I'd like to die someday. He went while serving others; I can't think of a better way to go. This thought occurred to me not too long ago as I laid flat on my back on the kitchen floor of the shelter where I volunteer now. The shelter's freezer door was cracked open and ice had built up on the floor. I was working in the kitchen and walked over toward the freezer when I slipped on the ice and had a terrible fall. I got pretty banged up and could have easily hit my head on the cement and died right there. As I sat on the floor rubbing my new goose egg, I thought of Paul and realized it wouldn't have bothered me at all to die at that moment, because I was following his example in helping my sisters and brothers. There was an undeniable sense of peace in that realization.

## — LEARNING TO TAKE CARE OF MYSELF TOO —

As incredible as life was in the late 1990s and into the 2000s, it wasn't all picture perfect. Sure, my business experienced tremendous growth during that decade, and the years I spent serving the CCEDA gave me the chance to help more people in more ways than I ever imagined. And, of course, my family thrived in Hartford. Gail settled into a wonderful career as a highly respected engineer in the aeronautics industry. At one point, about 2,000 engineers worked under her. She probably worked as many hours as I did all those years! And our daughter, Crystal, exceled in her studies and grew into a fine young woman.

Despite all the success I'd had and continued to have during that time, the years after Paul's death were the darkest times of my life—and, considering how I spent the first twenty years of my life, that's saying something. With so much change and so many responsibilities building up in such a short span of time, not to mention the years of abuse and emotional damage I had only recently began to fully unpack, I must admit that a deep depression settled over me. It was during this season more than any other, I think, that God was teaching me how to take care of myself. And, after spending so much time and energy helping others, I realized that I needed to learn how to let others help me.

Gail and Crystal were crucial during this time. Their presence always lifted my spirits and helped me focus on the good things in life. Gail is a devout Christian woman, so one of the first things on her list when we arrived in Hartford was finding a church for our family to attend. We went to the Northside Church of Christ the very first week Gail joined me in Hartford and were soon attending twice a week, on Wednesdays and Sundays. By then, we were financially comfortable, and you could tell by our neighborhood. It was the polar opposite of the dingy apartment I lived in before Gail and Crystal moved from Detroit. We bought a house in a nice area of town, and Crystal attended a school that was predominately white. That made our church home—a mostly black congregation—even more important to us. Even while attending a white school and living in a largely white neighborhood, Crystal was still raised with a good sense of her black culture.

Gail's strong Christian faith and dependence on God was a powerful force for good in our family. She prayed for me every day, and I knew it. Her faith fueled my own, and my relationship with God proved to be the most powerful source of strength and security for me as I continued to fight depression. I developed a habit of daily prayer and meditation that is still a high point of my day. I spend an hour or two every morning praying and meditating. I turn on some of my favorite spiritual music and simply talk to God. I tell Him everything, and I give Him a chance to talk back while I listen. It's hard for anyone to sit still long enough to have a meaningful time of meditation with God, but I don't think I would have made it through that season without it. That quiet time is like my daily medicine. No matter how crazy the days get or how painful life can be, I make it a priority. It's the time I've set aside each day to soothe my mind and let myself believe that everything's going to be okay.

Depression is hard to describe to people who don't understand it. It's like you're trapped inside a cylinder, trying to climb out by pressing your hands and feet against the sides and inching your way up. But the thing is, someone's at the top pouring oil all down the sides. You're trying so hard to push yourself up, but you just keep sliding further down into darkness. You know there's joy at the top of the cylinder, but you just can't make it there.

This isn't a book on depression, and I won't go into my own journey through it in detail. However, if you know what I'm talking about and haven't gotten help, please learn from my mistakes and talk to someone right now. I waited far too long before ever sitting down with a therapist. It wasn't because I didn't think I needed it; it was because I was scared of it. Therapy can be terrifying, because you know you're going to have to open old wounds and unpack the years of baggage you've tucked away and hidden in the dark parts of your heart.

When I finally gave therapy a try, I stumbled a lot. I'd always preferred to run away and hide those wounds rather than deal with the scars. But I've realized it's important to know yourself, so you can recognize when you're really sliding back down that cylinder again and need some help.

I've been blessed to help a lot of people through a lot of different hardships over the years. The hardest person to help, though, has been myself. It was always easier to focus on someone else's problems, someone else's needs, someone else's junk. Think about the little speech you always hear when you get on an airplane. In an emergency, they tell you right up front to put the oxygen mask on yourself *first* before you try to help anyone else. I used to think that was crazy. I thought, *Why would I help myself before I help someone else, especially my own child?* Now I know better. What I discovered through prayer, meditation, and lot of therapy is that I can't be much good to anyone else if I'm falling apart inside. By taking care of myself, I know I'll be around to serve others for a long, long time. And I can serve them even better when I'm doing it from a place of mental and emotional strength.

The decades I spent in Hartford taught me how to serve other people in small, personal ways and in gigantic, city-changing ways. Those years also taught me how to take care of myself. Professionally, personally, socially, and philanthropically, Hartford had become my home, and I never thought I'd leave. But I'd soon learn there were more people to help, and there was at least one more major move in my future.

My life was about to get shaken up once again.

## EIGHT

# Another Move, Another Mission

*"Truly I tell you, whatever you did for
one of the least of these brothers and
sisters of mine, you did for me."*

~ MATTHEW 25:40 ~

By the late 2000s, I'd had a few big changes in my life. I had continued to fight the long, hard battle against depression, unpacking all the trauma from my childhood. Also, Gail and I were no longer married by then. She is and always will be the love of my life and my dearest friend; in fact, she's still the executor of my will and trust, and I couldn't trust her more. Though it was painful for both us, we knew it was the right decision for where we were in life. And, of course, Crystal was grown and gone. Of all the changes at this stage of my life, that's probably the one that stung my heart the most.

## — CATCHING UP WITH CRYSTAL —

My daughter has always been a marvel. We never experienced "the terrible twos," I never heard her utter a single curse word, and she never had a drop of alcohol as a child. And she spent practically all her free time serving other people—particularly the deaf community. You can imagine how proud I was to see her prioritize service. Crystal was always a hard worker and never that concerned with money, either. If I added up every dollar she ever asked me for, it wouldn't even total $2,000. She was shocked and cried when I gave her a car on her sixteenth birthday. She thought Gail and I were being nice. The truth is, we were just glad we didn't have to drive her around to all her volunteer commitments anymore!

**If I added up every dollar she ever asked me for, it wouldn't even total $2,000.**

I wasn't worried about boys or an unwanted pregnancy, either. Before a young man could ever even get to *me*, they first had to pass Crystal's own impossibly high standards. She only had one boyfriend in high school, but even that didn't last very long. She broke up with him as soon as she realized he wouldn't go to church with her.

It became clear early on that she possessed a remarkable intellect too. She started reading at only eighteen months! When they gave her the standard school tests in kindergarten, they discovered she was a full two years ahead, so she skipped the first grade. Even then, she took all honors classes and found them only mildly challenging. All through school, she never received any grade lower than an A.

At age sixteen, Crystal was accepted into the Ivy League Wharton School of Business. This is an extremely prestigious school. I recently heard a famous person bragging about how his children were accepted to Wharton. I'd love to meet that guy and say, "Wharton? Oh yeah, my daughter was accepted there—from a public high school with no extra tutoring—*when she was sixteen*." To her credit, though, Crystal turned Wharton down. Even though she was the sole heir to one of the most successful black-owned businesses in the country, she always knew she didn't want to follow me in the car business. She saw how hard I had always worked and how many hours I spent at my dealerships, and she wanted no part of it.

Besides, Crystal already knew what she wanted to do with her life. From the age of fourteen, she knew she wanted to become a doctor. She had always spent time volunteering with me at the Mercy homeless shelter, and she became especially passionate about serving the deaf. Most of her volunteer time in high school was spent at the American School for the Deaf in Hartford. This fueled her desire to go into medicine, as she wanted to one day discover a cure for deafness.

After high school, Crystal attended Northwestern University, the "Ivy League of the Midwest," which has one of the best schools of speech in the country. From there, she went on to attend the Mayo Clinic School of Medicine in Rochester, Minnesota. This is where she received an unexpected blessing from all the volunteer work she'd done throughout her life. Back in the 1950s, a doctor had established a scholarship at the medical school that provided a full-ride scholarship to one deserving student per year. The criteria? It was awarded to the student who had spent an enormous number of hours throughout their young life volunteering and serving the underprivileged. Once again, I saw providence at work. This time, however, it was working for my daughter. When it comes to volunteering, I guess the apple doesn't fall too far from the tree.

With school behind her, Crystal met and married a wonderful man—a pastor—and they now live in Texas with my only grandchild. Words can never express how thankful I am that God sent me Crystal, my gift from heaven, or how very proud I am to be her father. After a life spent with the lowest of lows and the highest of highs, Crystal has taken my view of life and love to a whole new level.

## — THREE Ds TO DESTINY —

y 2008, I was still regularly working twelve- to sixteen-hour days trying to build my business and serve my community. I was in my late fifties then, and I hadn't slowed down for one minute from the moment I started college. Forty years of momentum was about to catch up to me and maybe even roll right over me if I didn't make some changes, but I was too set in my ways to see the danger signs. Fortunately, the choice was about to be taken out of my hands.

All I'd known for several decades was work-serve-work-serve-work-serve. Every day was about building my business and serving my community. It was a nonstop freight train pushing me forward every day. I guess if it were up to me, I would have ridden that train right into the ground. But then, three things happened in quick succession: a diagnosis, a departure, and a dream. I call them my "Three Ds to Destiny" because, taken together, it was an undeniable sign that God was shaking things up for me. He had more work for me to somewhere else. But first, He had to get me to let go of my crazy, hectic life in Hartford.

## A Troubling Diagnosis

My mind has always been my secret weapon. I was blessed with an analytical mind and excellent memory, something I constantly exercised and developed through years of schooling, engineering practice, and real-world problem-solving. Maybe someone else wouldn't have noticed the symptoms: a missing key, a colleague's name, a common word that's just out of reach. Most people probably struggle with these things every day, but I never had. No matter what was going on in my life, I never once doubted my mind or memory. That's what made these little slipups so apparent to me right away.

I was worried. I still felt young; I wasn't even sixty, but it seemed like every time I turned around, there was another news story about memory loss and early onset Alzheimer's.

I called my doctor, who ordered all kinds of tests. By the time they were done, I'd seen four different doctors and had tons of blood work, brain scans, sleep studies, memory tests, the works. They all came to the same conclusion: there was no physical reason for my sporadic mental lapses. Everything was working just fine. But, after working all day every day, seven days a week with no breaks, my problem seemed pretty clear to the neurologist. He put it simply, "Tony... you've fried your brain."

I'm a car guy, so I understood it in car terms. I knew that even the finest sports car would eventually break down if it was driven too far, too fast, without proper maintenance. My brain had always been my engine. People I worked with had given me nicknames like Brains and Human Calculator. But I had been neglecting the proper maintenance. I'd been running on fumes for years, and my mind was finally starting to show some wear and tear.

> **I'd been running on fumes for years, and my mind was finally starting to show some wear and tear.**

It was a moment of reckoning. I'd always depended on my mental stamina to get through a demanding daily schedule of challenge after challenge. I started to wonder if all the stress and pressure was worth it. How many dealerships did I have to own before I could call my business a success? How much money did I have to make to feel satisfied? I had already made more money than I would ever be able to spend in my lifetime. So, what was I doing? How many mountains did I have to climb?

Hearing doctors use terms like "fried your brain" and "burnt out" was alarming, but the real wake-up call for me was the slight loss of mental sharpness. It became clear that, if I didn't make some big changes, I'd continue to lose my mind bit by bit. I wasn't okay with that. Adding ten more dealerships to my portfolio wasn't worth losing ten percent of my brainpower!

I realize now that this season of introspection and doctor appointments was the best thing that could have happened to me. The ambitious, type A part of me wanted to keep grinding it out, but the memory loss told me it was time to get off the hamster wheel and make a major change. But what?

### A Departure That Made Dollars and Sense

I gave myself some time to think about what I should do. I knew I could cut back significantly on my business activity. The truth is, the timing couldn't have been better. My dealerships were running efficiently under invested general managers who didn't require my constant supervision. There was really only one project on my list that needed my direct attention, and that was a new Honda dealership I'd recently built and staffed in Wesley Chapel, Florida, just north of Tampa.

A thought struck me from out of the blue: *What if I moved the corporate office to Florida?* This would allow me to personally get the Honda dealership off the ground and keep my executive position in the March–Hodge partnership, but I could systematically reduce my work hours, eliminate work-related travel, and give my fantastic management team a chance to step up.

As I explored this option, two other big benefits rose to the surface. First, this would get me back to the warm Florida weather I grew up in. It had been forty years since I left Florida for college in D.C., followed by General Motors in Detroit, and then my dealership business in Hartford. I had never gotten used to all the ice and snow I'd had to put up with for the past four decades. Getting back to Florida's year-round sunshine and short-sleeve temperatures would definitely be a perk.

The second benefit was the key factor, though, and that was the financial incentive. My accountant loved the idea of me moving from Connecticut to Florida, and he did his best to convince me how this could save me and my family a fortune. "Look at it this way," he said. "There's no personal income tax in Florida, and there's also no millionaire tax like we have in Connecticut. Moving there is like getting a 6 percent raise without doing anything. And, if you're living in Florida on the day you die, your family will inherit 12.5 percent more than they would if you lived in Connecticut." Well, I'm a numbers guy. Moving to Florida made dollars *and* sense. The decision was made. I brought a new home in Tampa and moved the corporate office—and my life—to Florida.

## A Dream to Live By

As always, once I made up my mind, I quickly started to follow through with the details. But, while I focused on the logistics of moving to Florida, a lingering doubt continued to buzz around inside my head. On paper, slashing the length of my workday was possible, but I already saw a potential problem. I had to be honest with myself: I knew I had an obsessive personality. I needed to stay busy. It was fine to say I would cut down on my business hours, but what was I going to do with all this extra time in my daily routine? I wasn't good at leisure. I didn't have hobbies, other than a round of golf every now and then. Always the introvert, I didn't have much of a social life (and I didn't really want one). What could I do?

The answer came from an unexpected source. It came to me in a dream just a few weeks after I settled into my new home in Tampa. I went to bed that night with the same routine I'd followed for decades, saying a quick prayer just as I felt myself drifting off to sleep. As a strong believer in God, I had become accustomed to speaking with the Lord in my prayers. But that night, He answered back.

I heard a voice speaking to me. I remember listening intently and then jolting awake. I jumped out of bed and wrote down every single word of what I heard Him say to me:

My son, I gave you hardship in your youth, so that when you went from poverty to plenty, you could understand the struggle of "the least of these." (Matthew 25:40)

My son, I helped you leap over hurdles as you became an entrepreneur. I rewarded your achievements with great wealth. Do not stand atop the highest peak of success and think of the things this wealth can buy. Turn around. Turn around and look back down the mountain. See your brothers and sisters struggling where you once were.

My son, it's time to Pay It Backward. Climb back down to the bottom. Help them see the top. Help them climb out of poverty and join you at the peak.

It was the missing piece from the puzzle of my life. Even after years of counseling, I'd never fully understood the misery of my childhood; I just couldn't find God's reasons for it all. But, in this dream, He explained why I had to suffer. It was the insight that put everything into perspective. I wrote down my thoughts:

> *I have been blessed by God.*
> *Blessed to grow up hungry every day.*
> *Blessed to have no one read a book to me.*
> *Blessed to move seventeen times as a child, including an orphanage stay.*
> *Blessed to not know my father.*
> *Blessed to have a mother who didn't give affection.*
> *Blessed to have no one attend my graduations.*

How can I call these blessings?

If I had not grown up without food, I would not know how it feels to be hungry.

If I had not moved seventeen times, I would not know how it feels to be homeless.

If I had not lived without a parent's love, I would not know how it feels to be unwanted.

God reminded me that night that I was a blessed man. And now, I was more excited than ever to share that blessing with others.

## A New Beginning

I woke up that morning with a clear understanding of how I needed to spend all that time I was freeing up—with service. There was no doubt that God was calling me to double down on my efforts to serve my community by getting even more involved and going even further to serve the least of these. That's a phrase that has meant a lot to me throughout my life. The one good thing I can say about my mother is that she taught us about God. That planted a seed of faith in me that God continued to grow throughout my life. My favorite Scripture passage has always been Matthew 25:40, where Jesus is talking about God's view of people helping other people. Using a parable, Jesus says, "Truly I tell you, whatever you did for one of the least of these brothers and sisters of mine, you did for me."

Throughout my career, I always fit in my charity work around my business life. It was time to turn that around. From this point on, paying it backward was going to be the thing that got me out of bed every morning. I knew serving others would be my mission for the rest of my time on this earth.

Two days after having my dream, when I had gathered my thoughts and had a good idea of what God was telling me to do, I called my daughter in California. I wanted to tell Crystal about my new long-term strategy for living my life. More importantly, I wanted to hear her say I was making the right choice.

We chatted for a bit at first, talking about our upcoming annual summer vacation, before she asked how I was settling into Tampa. "Well, I think I know what I want to do with my time," I said. "I want to devote myself to helping the least of these."

Crystal is every bit her mother's daughter, very familiar with the Scriptures. She knew exactly what I meant, and her voice lit up as she replied, "That's a great idea, Dad! It's a great way to live the rest of your life."

**She knew exactly what I meant, and her voice lit up as she replied, "That's a great idea, Dad! It's a great way to live the rest of your life."**

I felt a surge of joy as we said goodbye. The call was everything I'd hoped for. My future felt full of promise. Writers and philosophers, even behavioral scientists, talk about the "moment of truth" when a person realizes his or her purpose in life and commits to fulfilling it. For me, it was that dream. I had already given thousands of hours and generated millions of dollars to help the poor and the vulnerable. But now that God had shown me the connection between my terrible upbringing and my mission to serve, I was truly ready to do all I could.

Nearly twenty-five years earlier, in 1994, I had created a foundation for charitable giving. For lack of a better name, I called it the Tony March Foundation. But my dream inspired me and gave me a new focus, and I wanted the name of the foundation to reflect that. Soon after, I legally changed its name to the Pay It Backward Foundation. It was a better representation of what God had placed in my heart.

Inspired by God's words and my love of service, I wanted to spend the rest of my days making the Pay It Backward Foundation the best it could possibly be. I thought back to Hartford's Mercy homeless shelter and Paul Laffin. I wanted to spend my days like him, meeting the homeless on their terms and helping them through their struggles. But the Mercy shelter I knew and loved was now twelve hundred miles away from me. That meant I had to find a new place to serve.

## — METROPOLITAN MINISTRIES, MY NEW HOME BASE —

It didn't take me long to find my homeless shelter. Metropolitan Ministries is a much bigger operation than I was used to at Mercy in Hartford. In fact, Metropolitan Ministries serves the entire Tampa Bay region. In 2016, they had a $23 million budget, which gave homeless families a collective 174,639 nights off the streets

while providing practical help to 27,616 families.
Metropolitan Ministries provides 1.3 million meals every
year, each distributed by one of twenty-eight different
organizations around the city. Most importantly, more than
five hundred children receive help from Metropolitan
Ministries every single day. I knew immediately that this
would be my new home base for serving the community.

### A Full Menu of Services

One of the most exciting things about Metropolitan
Ministries is the variety of programs and opportunities
it provides to Tampa's homeless population. One of the
shelter's many innovative programs is UPLIFT, a year-long
course of life skills. The goal of the program is to help
residents gain self-sufficiency and stay off the streets, and it
has an incredible 93 percent success rate of graduates staying
off the streets for good. Program participants receive help
with job searches, interviewing skills, culinary training,
financial counseling, anger management classes, and more.
Again, true change comes when you teach people how to
fish instead of just handing them a fish. At Metropolitan
Ministries, we do plenty of both: we serve more than a
million meals a year but, by teaching those people how to
fish, we ensure many of them eventually leave the shelter
and never return.

I work at the main Metropolitan Ministries campus,
which occupies an entire city block in a mixed-use

neighborhood. That basically means they've found a balance between urban decay and urban renewal. Of all the available programs, I was most drawn to their Inside the Box initiative. Its slogan is "Good food doing good," and it's designed to fund ministry operations through food-related services. Through Inside the Box, we take daily lunch orders for sandwiches, soups, and salads from throughout Tampa's corporate community. We also offer full catering services for big events, which we run out of the kitchen of the main campus. I was blown away the first time I walked into that kitchen. It's bigger than the entire Mercy shelter in Hartford! More impressive, it's bigger and better equipped than most commercial kitchens in hospitals and hotels. On a busy day, we can turn out six thousand meals. The soup vat alone is impressive. The first time I saw it, my jaw hit the floor and said, "That's all soup? Two grown men could fit in that vat!"

Additionally, Inside the Box runs small shops in downtown Tampa called Dough Nation, which sell cookie dough. And we have a growing list of grab-and-go locations at the Orlando and Tampa airports, another at the *Tampa Bay Times* building, and one in the downtown Armature Works building. With my passion for feeding the homeless, I love that Metropolitan Ministries found a way to monetize food services to help feed and shelter Tampa's homeless families. I thought it was a brilliant business idea!

Most impressive to me is that Metropolitan Ministries started its own Culinary Arts School. The sixteen-week program is free to all its residents and anyone else from the community that wants to learn how to become a certified chef. This program has been highly successful in transitioning people out of homelessness and giving them an unexpected career in the dining industry. Metropolitan even works with local restaurants to place its graduates into good-paying jobs. Many also complete their training and stay with Metropolitan as employees and instructors.

The irony of starting my life in misery in the Black Box and then, decades later, volunteering my time at Inside the Box is not lost on me. Neither is the fact that in both cases, I was surrounded by the least of these. The difference is, then, I was one of them; now, I'm trying to help them become one of me.

## A Day in the Life

Since I moved to Tampa in 2008, I've worked to rebalance the ratios of work and life. I've gradually spent less and less time on business and more time on charity, until, in 2015, I finally reached my goal of spending only half of a normal work week on the business and the other half volunteering. There are always exceptions, like when I'm traveling, but the scales have tipped for good. I've now transitioned to a life of service. Writing checks always made me feel good, but being involved myself, making personal connections, and getting my hands dirty while making a difference is the most rewarding work I've ever done. My heart is light.

People often ask me what a typical day looks like for me now. Although there's always a surprise or two, I can tell you how it usually goes. I arrive at the shelter by 8:00 a.m. and head up the back ramp into the kitchen area wearing my staff shirt with an embroidered Inside the Box patch. Many days, my job at the shelter is like a utility infielder, filling in wherever I'm needed—and someone *always* needs help because it's an enormous, busy place. We're feeding all the ministry's staff and residents, providing food for twenty-eight offsite locations, filling takeout orders, and preparing food for catering events. It's a madhouse half the time, but, hey, it's home.

From there, I'll usually walk down the narrow corridor lined with huge food freezers and check in on two food preparation rooms. It might seem loud and crazy to an outsider, but I can tell when everything is going well. If they don't need an extra set of hands, I'll head to the dishwashing bay. This is where I found a pile of work waiting for me one day recently. Every available surface was covered in haphazard piles of unwashed pots, pans, and utensils. That's when I knew I found my big job for the day. I rolled up my sleeves and dug in.

Believe it or not, it took six hours for me to get to the bottom of that pile of dirty dishes. Like I said, Metropolitan Ministries goes through a *lot* of pots and pans in a day. I found out near the end of my shift that the dishwasher had called in sick for his shift that morning. That could have been a disaster. A lot of people would have had their day ruined if the massive Metropolitan Ministries kitchen had ground to halt just because of a pesky pile of dishes. The staff would have been in a pinch, the residents might have missed a meal, and orders might not have gotten filled, which would have cost the ministry money from missed deliveries. Make no mistake about it: washing dishes is good, honorable, important work. I'm so glad I was there and able to pitch in.

The kitchen is always a lot quieter near the end of my shift. The volunteers—a mix of high school students, court-ordered people fulfilling their community service credits, and regular people doing their weekly charity work—are already gone. As I walk back through the kitchen, I run into other people wrapping up their own shifts. Some of them are paid staff members, and others are residents who work shifts to be able to stay at the shelter.

**I felt closest to my calling when I was just quietly doing my work.**

I've become familiar with some of the staff, but I generally keep to myself. Once an introvert, always an introvert, I guess. Besides, I actually didn't *want* the people I served with at Metropolitan Ministries to get to know me. I didn't want them to know about the big checks I wrote or about my successful career, and I *definitely* didn't want anyone to make big announcement about a gift or have people standing around me clapping. That sounds like a nightmare to someone like me. I wasn't there for any of that. I didn't need it, and I didn't want it. Sure, I gave money to Metropolitan Ministries—a lot of money, in fact—but I did it privately for the longest time. When I was there working, I only wanted to be known as a committed volunteer. I felt closest to my calling when I was just quietly doing my work, helping out wherever I could and wherever they needed me. I just wanted to be the Tony who could always lend a hand during a shift, prepare some meals, do the dishes, and clean the bathrooms. And I was afraid they wouldn't ask me to sweep the floors if they knew my whole story.

## Outside the Shelter

I was so happy to have found my new routine at Metropolitan Ministries, but I still love it when providence gives me a random opportunity to lend a hand, especially with kids. I'll always have a soft spot in my heart for helping needy children.

One day on my commute to the shelter, I saw a group of boys wearing football jerseys soliciting money for their team at a busy four-way intersection. I gave one of the kids a $100 bill, and I laughed as I heard him shout out to his friends about the donation he scored. I got one block down the street before I felt an urge to go back and talk to the boys. I pulled into a parking lot, parked my car, and walked back to the intersection. I had a gut feeling I should hear more about them.

These seemed to be fine young men. We talked about school and the importance of keeping studies a priority, something I always stress to students whenever I talk to them. A few minutes later, their coach saw us talking and walked over. He assured me the boys had to do well in school to stay on the team and explained they were collecting money for new uniforms so they could play in the local youth football league.

Once he mentioned that, I did notice that the boys' helmets were showing some wear. The coach admitted that concussions were always a concern in football—more so with outdated equipment. That sealed the deal for me. I asked the coach to send me a complete list of equipment the team needed to be properly outfitted, and his list arrived a few days later. I wrote out the check for $6,000 to ensure those boys and their brains would stay healthy and strong for another few seasons.

That moment (and many others like it) is why I've worked so hard my whole life. I've never been worried about having more than everyone else. I've never kept up with the latest technology or toys, and I don't have expensive tastes. I don't mind using an old phone or watching an old TV if it means I get to ease a hard-working coach's mind and give kids the confidence to play sports without getting hurt. Forget the flashy toys; *that's* my big-ticket item right there. That kind of spending puts a smile on my face, when I feel my charity gene kicking in.

## — POKER VERSUS POVERTY —

said earlier that I never really had much in the way of
hobbies. My work schedule, volunteer activities, and
family commitments kept me busy, so I never had any
time left over for learning to play an instrument or shooting
hoops. That started to change one night in 2010. I came
home after an especially busy day working at the shelter,
which was a bit more hectic than usual. While I was there,
I had to stop several times to deal with some problems at
one of my dealerships. My phone rang in my pocket every
half hour with something that needed my attention. By the
time I got home, I was beat.

I fell into my chair and started flipping through TV
channels, just trying to find something to help my brain
calm down after a crazy day. I came across an episode of
the World Poker Tour, with six players vying for a million
dollars in a game of no-limit Texas hold'em. I had never
played poker, but I was quickly pulled into the action
and realized something as I watched the master players at
work. Unlike casino gambling, which featured *negative
expectation* games—games that were mathematically
impossible to beat in the long run—poker offered the best
player a *positive expectation* of winning. In other words, luck
wasn't a huge factor in winning at poker. Sure, luck played
a role, but a skilled poker player would always come out
ahead of a less-talented opponent in the long run. That
explained how professional poker players, who invested

themselves in the game full time, could actually make a living at it. I was intrigued.

## Mastering the Game

Poker involves a firm grasp of key mathematical principles, so I was drawn to it immediately. I learned to approach a hand of poker like an engineer facing an electrical challenge, processing the information at hand to make deductions and choices that gave me the best chance of solving the problem. In this case, that meant winning the hand.

Starting that night in front of the television, I fell hard into the poker rabbit hole. I set my DVR to record any poker shows available, subscribed to the World Poker Tour online, and studied books about poker by experts like Phil Hellmuth and Gus Hansen. I played online poker for free and spent hours late into the night studying the players' moves on TV. I found it all fascinating, and it grew into an enjoyable hobby. The intricacies of each hand and the logic involved in solving the poker puzzles took me right back to my middle school days when I first discovered my love for math. It was a perfect way for me to quiet my mind after a busy day of work and volunteering. In fact, it felt like meditation, designed specifically for me.

There was a time when players relied on hunches, intuition, and the basic strength of their hand to win. Most were uninterested in the critical mathematical

component of the game, and many were completely
unaware of it. That's all changed in recent years. Today,
players focus on honing their mathematical skills to play the
game successfully. With my background in math, including
advanced calculus, differential equations, probability theory,
and statistics, I was in my element at the poker table. And
I wasn't the only one. I realized many of the top young
players around me had attended math-focused schools such
as MIT, Caltech, and Stanford.

During the two years I spent learning the game, I
never once played for money. I wasn't looking for a game
of chance, so I knew I needed to hone my skills at safe
(and free) poker tables. By the time I felt ready to compete
for real, I was well-versed in every aspect of the game. I
understood winning hands through pot odds, implied odds,
reverse and expected equity, and fold equity. I wouldn't
expect you to understand those terms if you aren't a poker
player yourself, but I was shocked to realize that many of the
players around me didn't understand them either. Almost
every poker table includes several people who simply don't
understand or even notice the importance of math in the
game they're playing. There's a name for those players:
*dead money.* These are the men and women who flat-out
hand over their cash to more knowledgeable players in the
game—players like me.

At sixty years old, I found yet another good use for
my natural aptitude for math. I started winning, and I
never looked back. As I won more and more, though, an

old, familiar question popped into my head: *What should I do with all this money I'm winning?* My car dealerships had provided me with all the money I'll ever need, so I decided to get creative with my new poker hobby. I decided then and there that this happy accident—my newfound love of poker—would fit perfectly into my mission to pay it backward. I decided right at the start to donate all my winnings to charity.

## Chips for Charity

Discovering poker was a revelation for me. As crazy as it sounds, I found a tremendous amount of peace at the tables. It became a form of therapy; I put my headphones on with the same spiritual music I start my day with and get lost in the music and the math. I wouldn't recommend this as a form of therapy for everyone, but it works for me. Even my counselor is on board.

Beyond the benefits I personally take away from the game, the idea of playing poker to benefit other people was exciting to me. It was an unexpected, even providential, way to combine my old passion (serving others) with my new passion (playing poker). Sitting at that table, I can be alone with God, clear my mind, give my brain an enjoyable problem to solve, take a break from work, get out of the house, and help other people all at the same time. Poker may be a terrible vice for many people, but, for me, it was a dream come true!

My accountant wasn't as excited about my new enterprise as my therapist was. He was understandably worried that I'd get carried away into a life of gambling, but he soon realized that's not what I'm about. He and I worked together to come up with a solid financial plan for my new income stream. Not only would I donate all my poker winnings to charity, but I decided not to deduct any expenses I incurred as part of the game. That meant any registration fees, travel, lodging, and so on came out of my pocket, while every dollar I won went straight into the Pay It Backward Foundation to help people break through the poverty cycle and start their own climb up the mountain of success.

**From that moment on, I couldn't play poker without thinking about the number of children I could feed if I won the money on the table.**

It was a turning point for me. From that moment on, I couldn't play poker without thinking about the number of children I could feed if I won the money on the table. I was always doing that math alongside the math of the game. I knew each meal Inside the Box gave to a hungry person cost $1.96 to prepare. So, if I won a $5,000 pot, I'd be buying lunch for twenty-five hundred kids. It was an incredible motivator. When I walked towards my table at a tournament, I'd imagine children from the shelter lined up along my path. Before each play, I'd imagine myself looking into their faces and remind myself to make the right choice because those kids were depending on me.

Hungry children weren't the only things I visualized as

I played. Poker had reignited my passion for math, and with that came a flood of fond memories of my HAWK teachers. I imagined them watching over me and guiding me through my games. Every player has some kind of strange superstition or ritual, and mine was centered around my HAWKs. I looked for their initials in my surroundings whenever I sat down to play. For example, when I played at the Seminole Hard Rock Hotel & Casino, the H stood for Mrs. Harris, the A represented Mrs. Aumiller, and the K was for Mrs. Keyes. It was harder to find Mrs. West in that one until I realized I could just turn the M in "Seminole" upside down. Once I flipped it around in my mind, I saw the W for Mrs. West clear as day, and I was ready to play.

If I found all their initials, I could settle my nerves and have a good day. If I needed a little extra help at some tables, I'd imagine my four teachers as hawks flying over to my opponents, landing on their shoulders, and making sure they didn't do anything to make me lose the hand. It may sound a little silly, but the strategy of visualization was something that had served me well in other areas of my life, so it felt perfectly natural to me when I applied it to poker. Thinking about the HAWKs and enlisting their help allowed me to concentrate and avoid distractions. It always seemed to work.

Once my games were dedicated to caring for hungry children and not just playing for fun or money, I really wanted to improve my skills. Soon, in addition to playing the cards I was dealt, I also started playing table position, stack size, and bet sizing to increase my winnings. Most importantly, I lifted my eyes and began to study the behavior of other players, watching how they bet and learning their mannerisms and tells to help me predict what kinds of cards they were holding. That's when the most elusive aspect of poker became clear to me. The introvert in me finally realized that poker isn't only about getting good cards and making good mathematical predictions; it's also about reading people. After such a long and successful career as an engineer and business owner, I was blown away by how many important new skills poker was teaching me.

## The Tourney Journey

Early on, I began playing tournament poker, where dozens, hundreds, or even thousands of players compete against each other to be the last player standing. The winning players receive big money from the entry fees of players already knocked out of the tournament.

I won my first tournament in June 2012, two years after first stumbling upon a poker tournament on TV. It was a senior's event for players fifty years of age and older. A year later, I had an even bigger win, a second-place finish at a regional World Poker Tour event. That tournament won the Pay It Backward Foundation more than $62,000. The ball just kept rolling and gathering speed from there. By 2017, I'd made more than $500,000 playing tournament and cash poker for charity. In Inside the Box terms, that's about two hundred fifty thousand meals to help feed homeless citizens worldwide.

It wasn't long before I spent a good part of each year traveling to different tournaments. I even traveled to Melbourne, Australia, every January for their big Aussie Millions tournament. As I spent time in each new city, especially the ones I frequented on the tournament trail, I got to know the local homeless shelters and spent time learning about the different homeless communities across the country and around the world. I always loved hearing each shelter's unique approach to solving the problems of poverty, hunger, and homelessness. Poker gave me a wonderful opportunity to widen my perspective and see firsthand what other communities were doing to serve the least of these.

In 2017, I was in Las Vegas to play in the main event of the World Series of Poker. The entry fee was $10,000, and the winner would receive a whopping $8,000,000 pot. I was excited to play for such high stakes, but I came down with a severe ear infection the night before the event began. My doctor insisted I skip the tournament and fly home to get immediate medical attention. I reluctantly agreed, disappointed I'd have to miss my shot at winning such a huge pot for the foundation. My trip wasn't a total loss, though. On my way to the airport, I stopped by the event office and redeemed my $10,000 entry fee. I then went to the Las Vegas Rescue Mission, a shelter I'd visited many times. I met with the CEO of the shelter and gave him a check for $10,000 before I left. I wasn't in Vegas for fun or to get rich; I was there to earn money for charity. Even though I couldn't play the tournament,

I felt I should at least give the $10,000 I'd already planned to spend on that trip.

The shelter CEO was amazed and so, so grateful by the unexpected windfall. That much money goes a long way in local homeless shelters and missions, and it felt wonderful to invest in the communities where I was regularly playing cards. That spur-of-the-moment gift started a trend. Now, when I travel to play poker for charity, I always give a portion of my winnings to a shelter in the host city, so that local community can benefit from what I won there. The remainder, of course, goes to the Pay It Backward Foundation.

## — POKER BLEW MY COVER —

oker was certainly never on my radar, and I never expected a fun card game to open up a whole new world of philanthropy for me, but it has been a match made in heaven. Getting involved in the poker community and enjoying the brilliance of the game has been a much needed outlet for me. More importantly, it's been a blessing to a lot of people through the money I've won. I can't picture a better outcome from such a fun new hobby.

That said, I never imagined when I first started playing the game that poker of all things would be the thing that blew my cover as a philanthropist. All these years, I'd done my giving in relative anonymity while I donated my time to the shelter. There was really nothing to connect the guy who signed the big checks from the Pay It Backward foundation to the guy who cleaned dirty dishes at Metropolitan Ministries. That delightful separation came to an end in 2016 when I won a poker tournament that changed my life forever. I'll tell you all about it in the next, and final, chapter.

# NINE

## Out of the Box

*"To whomever much is given, of him will much
be required; and to whom much was entrusted,
of him more will be asked."*

~ LUKE 12:48 (WEB) ~

he house I bought when I first moved to Tampa in
2008 came fully furnished. Everything in the
home—all the furniture and décor—was picked out
by someone else. It helped take a lot of the stress out of the
relocation for me back then, but by 2015, I was ready to
make my home my own. So, I made plans to completely
redecorate. Of course, that meant getting rid of all my
furniture. As I walked through my house taking a mental
inventory of everything, I realized this could be a wonderful
opportunity to help the shelter. I decided to empty the whole
house and give everything to Metropolitan Ministries, who
could either use the furniture at the shelter or sell it to keep
the proceeds. This quickly became a bit more complicated
than I expected.

This would be a big donation and would require
some moving trucks and movers to help, so I decided to
reach out to the shelter's CEO, Tim Marks. Believe it or
not, I had never met Tim in the six years I'd served at

Metropolitan Ministries. A huge organization like that
has a lot of moving parts, and I was usually buried at the
back of the kitchen doing my best to stay under the radar.
But I figured I should call and talk with him about my
donation. I knew a gift this big and complicated would get
his attention eventually, and I wanted to get ahead of it and
still try to remain anonymous.

Tim is not the kind of a person to turn down a
contribution to the shelter. However, he had never received
this kind of request before. If purchased new, the contents
of my home would have exceeded $250,000. It was a *lot*
of stuff. The one luxury I've allowed myself over the years
is a beautiful home. After so many years of poverty and
instability in my home life growing up, I still get a sense
of calm and safety when I walk through my door at the
end of a day. It's bright and spacious, and it has a feeling
of permanence—all the things I didn't have growing up.
However, from Tim's perspective, he was just talking to a
random volunteer who mopped the kitchen floor a few days
a week. I got the feeling he wasn't really convinced that I
was serious.

As Tim and I talked by phone, we both realized he just
needed to see what we were dealing with instead of trying
to wrap his head around it over a phone conversation. So, I
invited him to my home the next week to check it out. A
week later, Tim and two of his staff members arrived, and
I could tell they were excited from the moment I greeted
them at the door. I guess seeing my house in person cleared

up any doubt and confusion he felt. After walking through the house, Tim and his staffers gratefully accepted my offer and decided to sell the furniture through two consignment stores and then keep the money for the ministry. When all was said and done, it took five truckloads to move everything out of my house and to the shops.

As Tim and I worked together to organize the donation, he started asking me a lot of questions about myself. I told him my story—the same story I've told you—and how much I loved being able to give both my time and money to charity. I reiterated, though, that I like to keep the two separated. I stressed that I wanted the gift to remain anonymous and I didn't want anyone at the shelter to really know who I was or what kind of home I lived in. Tim agreed and promised to keep the details secret, but I could tell I was officially on Tim Marks' radar from then on.

## — GETTING ATTENTION —

loved my shifts at the ministry. Arriving at the shelter felt like coming home, and my charity gene always got charged up the second I walked through the door. When you write a check to a charitable cause, you may feel good for five minutes, and that's great. But, when you spend five hours making fifty trays of bacon or three thousand cheesecakes that will fill hungry stomachs, you feel good for a whole lot longer. I enjoyed the idea that I was helping the shelter in two ways. First, by the actual work I completed for them. I went home every night knowing that I personally made a difference in people's lives. Second, the federal government made a monetary contribution to Metropolitan Ministries for every hour of volunteer service it received. I imagined the government receiving a monthly invoice for my work, and I loved it.

But what truly filled my heart was the chance to make a personal connection, or when I could see the difference we were making for someone who was struggling. I remember one day I was taking a break outside the kitchen when I saw a woman with a baby, pushing two grocery carts up to the ministry's Outreach Center. Everything she owned was in those two carts. Her entire life fit in two baskets. I cried out of sadness and relief. I remembered that desperation, of course; at the same time, I was so relieved Metropolitan Ministries would take her in and give her a safe place to live. I wiped the tears off my face, got back up, and went back inside to keep working. I was going to make sure that brave woman had a good meal that night.

Sometimes, especially over the holidays, I worked myself to the point of exhaustion. Christmas and Thanksgiving are always difficult times at the shelters. Like Paul Laffin always said, people living in the shelters are hungry every day. But, on those special days, we usually get a flood of new people hoping to get a free meal. Since the holidays are still an emotional time for me, even all these decades since my heartbreaking Christmases as a child, I try to stay busy during the season. That usually means working a lot of extra hours at the shelter.

One Thanksgiving, for example, I worked thirty-five hours over three days, with only a few hours of sleep a night to tide me over. And let's not forget that I was in my sixties by this point. On those days, I was not only preparing food but also breaking down the boxes, cleaning the floor, and hauling the garbage out to the collection bin. I laughed when I remembered what my teacher Mrs. Keyes said about catching me on a garbage truck and wondered what she would have thought if she'd seen me in that moment. By the end of the third day, standing and working on that unforgiving concrete kitchen floor, I was done. I used my last bit of energy to make it home and collapse into bed, where I stayed for the next sixteen hours straight.

I did my best to keep my head down and take care of whatever shift or task the ministry needed, but I soon realized my secret was starting to slip out. Tim Marks shared my story with the ministry's executive leadership, along with my desire to remain anonymous. As I worked more hours and was given more responsibilities by the volunteer leaders on the ground, the administration started having several conversations about me.

When Justine Burke, Metropolitan Ministries' marketing director, heard my story, she told her fellow administrators, "I have a job where I come to work and hear about people like Tony. That's my inspiration to carry on because I know there are people out there just like him who sacrifice so much to serve the homeless and needy." She was describing what's often called the "ripple effect," or how one person's actions inspires another to do something, and then *that* person's actions inspires another person to do something, and so on. I certainly wasn't trying to be an inspiration to anyone. In fact, I was trying as hard as I could to stay in the background. But, as more people heard about who I was, what I was doing, and why I was doing it, more people felt inspired to crank up their own level of service. In the process, more hurting people were being helped.

**"Tony," he said, "I want you to picture your story as a rock falling in a pond."**

Tim was a firm believer in the ripple effect and talked to me about it often. He was convinced that my story could be a catalyst to encourage other people to open their hearts, not to mention their wallets. Tim asked me to think about the power of the ripple effect. "Tony," he said, "I want you to picture your story as a rock falling in a pond. Think of all the ripples that would go out in all directions. Think of how far and wide the impact could be." The more he talked about it, the more I wondered if he was right. Would other people be inspired to give just by hearing my story? Could I help more homeless people by going public than I could by working in the

shadows? I just wasn't sure, and I was reluctant to give up the
freedom of my anonymity. Also, I really didn't want to make
a show out of my giving. I didn't want the attention; I'd rather
have all the attention go to the hurting men and women on the
streets who need help. I wanted people to see *them,* not me.

To his credit, Tim didn't push me and always respected
my privacy and my boundaries. Looking back, I think Tim
was just playing the long game with me. As a poker player,
I should have recognized his body language changes.

Speaking of poker, as I mentioned at the end of the last
chapter, it was a poker game that ultimately served as the last
straw in Tim's ongoing push to have me share my story. In
2017, I won more than $24,000 in the annual Aussie Millions
tournament in Australia. I always gave one hundred percent
of my winnings to charity, and that time, I decided to give it
all to Metropolitan Ministries and my old shelter in Hartford.
When I handed the check to Tim, a strange look spread across
his face. It was surprise and excitement, of course, but there
was something more. Thinking about it now, I know exactly
what it was: resolve.

The time had come.

## — GOING PUBLIC —

 week after I handed the check to Tim, I got a call
from him asking me to come meet with him and his
marketing team, Justine and Areil. When I arrived at

his office and sat down, all subtlety and pretense flew out the window. "Tony," he said looking me in the eye, "I want you to go public with what you're doing."

I immediately launched into my list of reasons for staying unknown. Tim had heard all this from me before. Justine and Areil, however, gently cut me off and put a new spin on it for me. They suggested that I look beyond myself. They explained that they could use my donations to create even more donations. They said that publicizing my giving, not only in poker but as a millionaire contributing money and time, would motivate other wealthy people to do the same. The result would be exponentially increasing the value of my contributions, meaning many more hurting people would get the help they need while giving many more wealthy people the opportunity to participate. The whole circle of giving would increase, and all it would cost was a little bit of my privacy.

I had never thought about it like that before. I thought about the people around me, like my fellow poker players. There was my hero, Barry Greenstein, who was known as the "Robin Hood of Poker" because he'd given away millions of his winnings to charity. I knew other players had followed Barry's lead and started to make regular contributions to charity. Maybe if those same poker players knew I volunteered my time, in addition to writing checks, they might be encouraged to do the same.

And that was just the poker players, who weren't all necessarily made of money. What about the businesspeople I'd been surrounded by for decades? What about my neighbors in my affluent community? What if we showed people how to do what I felt God calling me to do years earlier, to come back down from the mountaintop to help others? The potential impact was staggering, and that's just counting the people I personally knew. Who knows what could happen if total strangers heard my story and felt inspired to give too?

**Who knows what could happen if total strangers heard my story and felt inspired to give too?**

I loved the thought of being part of a wide circle of giving, but I still didn't like the idea of being at the center of it. Not only did this cut against my natural introversion and need for privacy, but it was a real moral dilemma for me. The Bible teaches about humility in giving and how we're not supposed to make a big show when we make a donation. As a person of faith, I've set a few key Scriptures at the very foundation of how I live my life. One of those has been Matthew 6:2, "So when you give to the needy, do not announce it with trumpets, as the hypocrites do in the synagogues and on the streets, to be honored by others." I have always taken that teaching to heart. I never wanted to spoil my giving by turning it into a whole production. But now, Tim and his marketing team were asking permission to *out* me, to go public about my contributions and service to others. That sounded dangerously close to "trumpets" to me.

I didn't want the attention, and I cringed at the thought of journalists writing about me. But I was curious about the prospect of motivating others, and I could feel excitement stirring deep inside me. I imagined those kids lined up waiting for their meal at the shelter. If other people decided to lend a hand, I knew we could feed a lot more kids. And, if more people volunteered at more shelters throughout Florida and maybe elsewhere in the country, I knew even more hungry children would get the help, food, and attention they needed. I was starting to break.

Tim, sensing a crack in my wall, pressed forward. "It's not just wealthy people that will be inspired by you, Tony. Think about the children. Those young kids living in poverty, just like you did. They'll hear your story, and they'll learn that education and hard work got you where you are today. They'll be inspired to break free of poverty and make their own dreams come true."

As a longtime car salesman, I had to appreciate how well he was working this negotiation. Finally, he leaned over his desk and delivered his closer, "We're not exposing you and your story to get accolades, Tony. We're doing it to change lives for the better."

What else could I do?

I closed my eyes.

I said yes.

## — FRONT PAGE NEWS —

ustine and Areil immediately went to work on the marketing plan to get my story out. Soon after, they contacted the *Tampa Bay Times* newspaper, but they weren't sure if the paper would be interested. Even if they

did send a reporter, there was no way to know if the story
would ever make it to print. If the paper didn't bite, they said,
we'd try something else.

We didn't have to try anything else.

On Sunday, April 23, 2017, I woke up, made a cup of
coffee, and got the Sunday paper off my doorstep. When I
opened it, I was shocked to see my own face staring back at
me. I was on the front page of the newspaper, my picture
along with the feature article titled "Undercover Volunteer"
by staff writer Paul Guzzo.[4] After spending decades working
and giving in secret, I was front page news. My days as a
private philanthropist were over.

*The Tampa Bay Times* is the biggest newspaper in Florida
and one of the top five papers in the country. And I swear,
every person in the state read that story. Certainly, all the
people I worked with at Metropolitan Ministries, all my
poker competitors, all my employees, and all my neighbors
read it. In the first week alone, the article received over
one million views online. Later that same week, the paper
published a follow-up editorial praising my efforts. Standing
alone in my house, I could *feel* all those eyeballs on me. I felt
all those people reading my story, hearing about my life in
the Black Box and learning about what I'd done to help the
homeless and hungry. It was the most uncomfortable I've
ever been. I couldn't help but wonder if I'd just made the
biggest mistake of my life.

There was nothing I could do, though. The cat was

---

[4] Paul Guzzo, "Undercover Volunteer," *The Tampa Bay Times,* April 23, 2017, https://www.tampabay.com/news/
humaninterest/undercover-volunteer-wealthy-car-dealer-does-the-dirty-jobs-quietly-at/2321093.

out of the bag. The bell had rung. All I could do was pray, so that's what I did. Day after day, my daily meditation time was filled with prayers that I'd made the right decision, that at least a few people would be inspired to give, that there'd at least be enough of a response to make all this feel worth it.

A couple of weeks later, after the media buzz had died down a bit and life started to feel a little normal again, Tim called and asked me to swing by his office for a chat. When I got there, he handed me a big stack of thank-you cards from people who'd read the article and sent letters of appreciation to me care of Metropolitan Ministries. I read through many of them and was overtaken by the kindness and encouragement of strangers who'd read the article. I felt awkward about it, but it also felt good on some level. I'd grown up with a mother and family who never noticed or cared about anything I did; all I ever wanted was their attention. Now, people I didn't even know were saying such wonderful things about me. It was nice—but mostly awkward.

I thanked Tim for sharing the letters with me, and he said he wasn't done yet. He handed me another big stack of papers. These weren't letters, though; they were copies of checks. I realized I was holding a giant stack of donations people had sent to Metropolitan Ministries after reading the article about me. I flipped through them and was blown away by the sheer number of checks and some of the amounts written on them.

This was a *lot* of money, and it was all going to help the poor and needy people of Tampa.

As if this wasn't gratifying enough, my eyes froze on one check. In the memo line at the bottom, the donor had written, "In honor of Tony March." I flipped through the stack and saw another one just like it. And another. And another. That's when it hit me: these people were new donors. Most had never participated in serving the hungry or ministering to the homeless in any way. But now, they were donating to the cause. They had been awakened to the urgent crisis in their own community, and they had chosen to act for the first time. And they did it just because they read my story.

I broke down and wept right there in Tim's office. It had worked.

## — A YEAR IN THE LIFE OF PAYING IT BACKWARD —

Just like that, I moved into a whole new stage of philanthropy: inspiring others to give. Things really kicked into high gear at that point. It was like my mission God showed me when I first moved to Tampa was refined. Now it wasn't just about seeing what I could do myself; it was about encouraging other people to examine their own lives and find a way to create positive change in their communities. And man, has that kept me busy!

I've spent my time since then working in homeless shelters and playing poker around the world, just as I did before. But now, I'm also doing a lot of public speaking wherever I go to encourage others to give their time, talents, and treasures. On top of that, now that my name is out, different organizations keep giving me awards for philanthropy. That still makes my skin crawl on some level, but I force myself to accept the award for one reason: it gives me the chance to deliver a thank-you speech in front of large crowds of philanthropists, who in turn get to hear all about the Pay It Backward Foundation. This alone has increased donations to the foundation exponentially, allowing us to serve more people than ever.

People often ask me what a typical week or month looks like now that my cover's blown. As busy as I am, I don't keep a schedule set in stone; it's not like the fifteen-hour days I used to spend onsite at my car dealerships. I keep regular shifts at the shelter, but even that is often interrupted by my travel schedule and other fundraisers. The best I can do some mornings is to spend my morning meditation praying, "Okay, Lord. Who am I supposed to help today?"

While I can't really give a picture of a typical week or month, I can share some of the opportunities I had the first couple of years after going public. I spent a lot of time visiting different shelters around the world, participating in poker tournaments (and giving away my winnings), and trying to build up the Pay It Backward Foundation.

The article came out in *The Tampa Bay Times* on April 23, 2017. That June, I played in the Las Vegas World Series of Poker tournament. While my competitors were living it up on the strip, I was spending my time at the Las Vegas

Rescue Mission, a huge shelter for men, women, and children. That's when I learned about the large tent city of Las Vegas, where a large crowd of homeless people live on the street together. It's hard to imagine, but these people know about the excellent shelter just a few miles away, but they prefer to live on the streets. That's true in practically every city. Because shelters are highly regimented and have such strict rules on eligibility and sobriety, many people prefer to take their chances on the streets so they can live however they want.

When I heard about the tent city in Las Vegas, I rented a car and went for a visit, handing out bottled water and socks as I talked to people. Fresh socks are actually one of the most precious items you can give a homeless person. They're an essential part of staying healthy when you live on the street, but people almost never donate their unwanted socks. They just throw them in the garbage, thinking they're worthless.

Sitting on a curb just a few miles from the Vegas strip and listening to people talk about their situations while they put on their new socks saddened me. How is it possible that there could be such a big homeless problem in a city that sees people gamble $265 million every day? And how is it possible for those people to survive outside when the temperature hits 115 degrees every day? After all these years, I still don't understand it. I guess I never will.

In July, I visited another tent city in Oakland, California, when I was in town visiting my daughter and her family. Maybe it sounds strange, but I got the feeling there was a real sense of community there. They all watched out for each other and guarded each other's meager possessions when someone had to leave. I talked with two police officers who said they stopped by regularly to check in. They told me that, although there was an ordinance on the books that forbid places like these, city officials *suggested* that offers not enforce it. "As a matter of fact," one officer told me, "unless a homeless person was committing a crime, we could get in big trouble if we arrested him."

While in Oakland that month, I stopped by another homeless encampment by the railroad tracks at the San Francisco Bay. This was the most heartbreaking homeless

enclave I have ever encountered. It had an air of utter hopelessness. I parked my rental car in front of a row of little shacks made of discarded pieces of cardboard, wood, metal, and plastic. This was precisely the kind of place Paul Laffin always told me to avoid. I said a prayer as I got out of the car, asking God to watch over me as I got out to talk to some people there.

A huge man approached me, introduced himself as Messiah, and told me about his entire journey to homelessness. We had a conversation about solving the problem in Oakland, and he had a lot of impressive ideas. After a while, I headed back to my car to leave. I glanced back at Messiah as he walked

away, and I saw that he had been holding a large hammer
behind his back the entire time we were talking. I could hear
my dear mentor Paul scolding me, and I gave thanks to God for
keeping me safe.

The next day, I visited St. Mary Center, which took care
of the homeless elderly. Now, that's a population that makes
you want to close your eyes and turn away. Not only did they
have to worry about their safety when around other homeless
people but they also had to cope with the increasing health
issues that come with aging. Of course, those issues often
went untreated.

That was a painful visit, but it was a much-needed
reminder that the homeless community isn't just made
up of young adults and middle-aged men and women.
Sometimes, it's destitute people in their sixties, seventies,
and eighties.

In September, I was back in Tampa when Hurricane Irma
hit. Like everyone else on the western coast of Florida, I had
to decide whether to leave the state or take my chances in
Tampa. I realized my decision was easy and killed two birds
with one stone. The Metropolitan Ministries kitchen was
one of the safest places around, made entirely of cinder blocks

with no windows. I spent the two days of the storm at the ministry, working in the kitchen by day and sleeping in it by night. I stayed safe in the storm, and I managed to help a few people along the way—not a bad way to spend a hurricane.

Just one week later, I started on my latest passion: cooking school! After years in the kitchen doing what I could to help, I wanted to become a certified chef so I could cook a meal from start to finish for three hundred people in the shelter. If a chef called in sick, I wanted to be ready to step in. It wasn't just about filling empty stomachs, though. Remember, Metropolitan Ministries ran a large business out of that kitchen, and the revenue created there was a huge source of income for the ministry. We couldn't afford to go without a chef for a single day, so getting qualified to fill his shoes in an emergency was important to me. I graduated from culinary school in September 2018, completing one of my lifelong goals.

In October, my culinary classmates and I spent an entire day prepping all the food for the Tampa Bay Food Fight fundraiser. The best chefs from Tampa competed with St Petersburg's best. The winners were the audience members and the Metropolitan Ministries Culinary Arts School, which received all the proceeds. The program trains at-risk students for a career in the food-service industry, giving them an income to support themselves and their families. The Pay It Backward Foundation was one of the sponsors for the event, and it was a huge success. We raised more than $200,000 and had a wonderful, fun night of competition. It was a great way for me to combine three of my loves: Metropolitan Ministries, the Pay It Backward Foundation, and cooking!

That December, I spoke at Metropolitan Ministries' annual breakfast meeting with community leaders and the city council. I talked about the exciting work the Pay It Backward Foundation was doing to help the citizens of Tampa, and I encouraged them to get involved in the upcoming Joy of Giving Event, which is hosted by WWE superstar Titus O'Neil (also known as community leader Thaddeus Bullard). We held the Joy of Giving Event just a few weeks later, right before Christmas. Ten thousand children got to walk through an entire football stadium full of dolls, TVs, bicycles, remote control cars, sports memorabilia, and more for the eighth annual celebration that provides gifts for the underprivileged. There were free food, games, and entertainment for everyone, many of whom would not be able to celebrate Christmas on their own. That was a great day, and it reminded me how special the Christmas season is (and should be) for a child. I never wanted any child to experience the pain I felt at Christmas when I was their age.

A week later, on New Year's Day 2018, I woke up to another surprise in *The Tampa Bay Times*. The paper named me one of the most intriguing people in Tampa. That really surprised and humbled me. More than that, it excited me, because I knew it meant a lot more people would hear about the work we were doing at the Pay It Backward Foundation. Maybe they'd write checks. Even better, maybe they'd be encouraged to take a shift at their local shelters.

In January 2018, I took what's become one of my favorite trips of the year: my annual trip to Melbourne, Australia, for the Aussie Millions poker tournament. I've grown to love the city, and I've won good money there for the foundation in the past. This year, however, I got an extra special surprise. Someone stopped me on the street and said, "Excuse me, are you Tony March?" I said yes and asked if I knew him. "No," he said. I follow you on Twitter and read all about the work you do for the homeless. I thought I recognized you! It's so great to meet you!"

I was shocked. I've never been recognized in public for anything I've ever done, but here was a guy in Australia who knew me and had been inspired to get involved in serving others. Thinking about it now, I still can't believe it. But I took it as another sign of providence. If word was getting out on the other side of the world, it was surely God's way of showing me I'd made the right decision about going public.

When I'm not playing poker during my time in Melbourne, I've gotten used to serving at the Salvation Army shelter there. Seeing how they treat their homeless citizens is an eye-opening contrast to how we typically do things here in America. Take how they handle mealtime at the shelter, for instance. People sit down at tables, order from a menu, and are served their food by wait staff, giving them the same experience they'd have in a restaurant. It really gives them a nice sense of dignity, something the homeless rarely get from other people.

Back home, I was honored to receive the national Service to Mankind award from Sertoma International in February 2018. Sertoma is a wonderful organization dedicated to meeting the needs and improving the lives of those impacted by hearing loss. That April, the Tampa Bay Lightning hockey team gave me its Hero Award. The honor also came with a $50,000 donation to the Pay It Backward Foundation. That night, I gave a check for $40,000 to Metropolitan Ministries and another one for $10,000 to my new friends at the Abe Brown Ministry, a local organization that provides transition housing and education for people who are recently released from prison. That was a great way to wrap up my first year in the public spotlight since the *Tampa Bay Times* article came out.

Since then, I've been back to the Las Vegas Rescue Mission and the Oakland tent city multiple times. I also got more involved in the Salvation Army homeless efforts in Melbourne. The Pay It Backward foundation helped fund new transitional housing resources there, as well as a state-of-the-art bathroom for the homeless in January 2019. The organizers of the Aussie Millions tournament gave the foundation the honor of opening the tournament that month in recognition of the contributions we'd made to charitable causes in Melbourne. That gave me the opportunity to tell the high-rolling poker players about the deep needs in Melbourne and around the world, something I always take seriously.

The foundation's work in Melbourne hasn't been our only international outreach. In 2018 and 2019, I made six separate trips to Winnipeg, Canada, to get involved in the many homeless initiatives there. I got to know the good people at Siloam Mission, one of the largest shelters in Canada, as well as those at the Community of Hope food pantry, which provides meals for the hungry. I especially enjoyed getting familiar with Winnipeg's Teen Challenge, a one-year program for homeless teenagers dealing with substance abuse. We should all strive to do whatever we can to serve hurting and homeless children wherever we find them. Aside from my Canada trips, I also traveled to the Dominican Republic and Haiti in 2019 to help where I could in those struggling communities.

**I've seen the bad, and I see the good. And I tell you, I feel confident. I believe we can make this world a better place ... together.**

Closer to home, I've become more and more involved with the work of Abe Brown Ministries in Tampa. This organization provides outreach and counsel to families that have been broken by incarceration. They also work with recently released prisoners, helping them prepare for life after incarceration. Our foundation recently committed to fully funding Abe Brown's fifth house for recently released prisoners transitioning back to life outside the prison walls.

All these new relationships—plus our ongoing work
with Mercy shelter in Hartford, Metropolitan Ministries in
Tampa, and other local and national organizations—keep me
pretty busy these days. That's my life now. Every day, I talk
to a hurting person or see a need that seems insurmountable,
and it shakes me to the core. But then I meet someone
who's ready to commit to a life of giving or I discover a new
organization dedicated to serving the least of these with love
and compassion. I've seen the bad, and I see the good. And
I tell you, I feel confident. I believe we can make this world
a better place ... together.

## — NOW IT'S YOUR TURN —

I recently turned sixty-seven years old. Most people my
age are enjoying retirement (or at least thinking about
it), but I'm not ready to relax yet. Instead, I'm loving
my third career as a philanthropist. I feel like I have a new
lease on life. Every morning I wake up and pray, "Who can
I help today?" I want to make a difference, but more
importantly, I want to inspire others to do the same.

Telling my story has definitely added a new dimension
to my life. It has forced me to interact with more people,
and there's a new softness to the connections I make.
People open up to me and strangers become friends. I've
realized that, while not everyone had a childhood as rough
as mine, everyone understands how it feels to struggle and

everyone understands what it means to feel alone. Still, it's difficult for me to talk with people. I feel so much more comfortable working my shift in the kitchen at Metropolitan Ministries than working the room at a big fundraiser. I'm still uncomfortable with that, but that brings me to the point of this whole book: I want you to join me in feeling uncomfortable.

You see, in order for us to change the world for the homeless and the hurting, we have to change our own worlds a little bit. That means changing our habits and lifestyles. It means changing our priorities. And a little change brings a little pain. It's uncomfortable. But, if you're reading this book, hopefully you've been motivated to *do something*. And that probably means doing something *different*.

I want you to feel inspired and consider what you can do with your time, talents, and treasures. There are so many ways to give like there's no tomorrow. If you've never made a monetary donation to a charity, start there. It's the easiest way to make a difference. My passion is people who are homeless, vulnerable, and abused. I hope you'll join me in my cause. But, if something else speaks to you, go with it! Animals, education, disease, clean water—you name it; they all need your money too. And don't worry about what you can afford. Remember, it costs less than $2 to feed a child at our shelter. The same is probably true at your community's shelter. Every little bit helps.

Don't just stop at writing a check out of your normal income, though. There's so much more you can do. How about monetizing your passion? If the dogs in the local animal shelter break your heart, start a dog-walking business and give the proceeds to the shelter. If education is up your alley, tutor children and give the money to your local library. If you're a home baker, hold a bake sale and take your profits to a local shelter. I know firsthand they'll be happy to see you.

If you're a real big spender, take your checkbook everywhere you go. When you're off celebrating your good fortune in faraway places, spread the wealth. Every time I get off a plane, whether it's business, pleasure, or something in between, I write out a check or two for local organizations doing good things. I think of it like a little travel tax I put on myself, and it's become a natural part of my travel budgets.

Invite your friends and colleagues to join in. Listen, you can have fun when you're working for a good cause. Get creative. Have a swear jar at work. Compete in weight-loss or no-vice competitions. Have everyone throw $5 in the kitty every time the office's favorite song comes on the radio. Instead of dinner and drinks out on the town, have a potluck and give everyone's saved money to charity. You have dozens of opportunities every day to turn an everyday experience or encounter into something that can benefit the needy. You just have to look for them!

So, that's helping with your dollars. Now, let's push you just a little further outside your comfort zone. How do you typically react when a homeless person calls out to you on the street? Would you consider a smile? How about some eye contact and a cheery hello? Or, how about something totally out of the box: make a few peanut butter sandwiches every morning and hand them and a bottle of water out during your daily commute. It takes very little time and very little money. All it really requires is your attention.

No one wants to be on the street. They're scared, they're sad, and they're embarrassed. Some basic human kindness from a stranger can heal a lot of hurt. Remember, we're all on that mountain. Maybe you're walking past someone who's clawing their way up, but we're on the journey together. So, let's get in there and lend a hand. If someone's looking for work, help him write his résumé. Take a shift helping a single mom with her kids. And, of course I may be biased, but I definitely recommend putting on an apron and taking your local shelter's kitchen for a test drive. You may discover a love for cooking just like I did.

The more people I meet through the Pay It Backward Foundation, the more amazed I am by the unique gifts we've all been given. It's incredible to learn about the ways people give back. In fact, I've been so impressed that we've started collecting stories. Join us at www.payitbackward.love to read all the different ways people are making a difference. Be warned, though: after reading these stories, you'll probably be ready to jump in and write your own.

When I think of someone writing a great story, I can't

help but think of my longtime friend Cornelius Martin.
He was the smartest black car dealer I've ever known.
When he died in 2006, he owned fifteen auto dealerships
and, as a huge motorcycle enthusiast, a few Harley-
Davidson retail locations. What I loved most about him
was his commitment to philanthropy. He gave generously,
systematically, and constantly. He was truly an inspiration.

Cornelius didn't just challenge me to *give* more; he
challenged me to *live* more. While I never allowed myself
many luxuries except a nice home, Cornelius found a way
to appreciate the finer things in life without having it cut
into his passion for giving. He lived a huge life and didn't
hesitate to celebrate his success. He even
owned four private jets, and he could never
understand why I always flew commercial.
He'd just laugh at me and say, "Tony, I've
never seen a Brinks truck following a hearse.
You can't take it with you!"

**No one wants to be on the street. They're scared, they're sad, and they're embarrassed. Some basic human kindness from a stranger can heal a lot of hurt.**

My friend Cornelius gave freely to all
sorts of causes, like education, minorities,
and business development, and he lived a full
life. In fact, Cornelius spent all his time on
his passions—both giving and playing—and
ultimately died in a motorcycle accident.
Many would call that tragic, and it I suppose
it was. But it was also an inspiration. Cornelius lived—*and
died*—doing what he loved. He is my inspiration to do
the same for myself. I hope I'm lucky enough to die like

Cornelius, doing the thing I love most in the world: spending my days working at the local shelter and looking for any chance to pay it backward.

And when my time's up, I aim to die the way I was born: with empty pockets.

*If you would like to follow Tony's personal journey and story,*
*or would like to donate to The Pay It Backward Foundation, visit*

PAYITBACKWARD.LOVE

All proceeds generated from the sales of this book
will go to The Pay It Backward Foundation
for the purposes of serving the Foundation's global mission.

# ACKNOWLEDGEMENTS

Writing this book has been one of the most rewarding—and frustrating—projects of my life. This book never would have made it to publication if it weren't for the tireless efforts of:

*My co-author, Marvin Karlins, who spent
hour after hour at my side, listening as I recounted the most
painful, joyful, and exciting stories of my life.*

*My amazing associate writers, Krista Simonson and Allen Harris,
and manuscript editor, Jen Gingerich.*

*My publisher, Jonathan Merkh.*

*My friend and creative consultant, Ray Kuik,
as well as Ray's family who hosted me during several visits.*

*My book jacket designer, Todd Krostewitz,
whose cover design brought tears to my eyes the first time I saw it.*

*My deepest thanks and heartfelt appreciation to you all!*

# TONY
# MARCH

*— a snapshot —*

Rare Family Photo: Nephew Byron, twin brother Bernard, Tony, and brother Gus

Football in High School –
The NFL might have to wait.

# Tony March is science award winner

**By LAURETTA ROSE MURPHY**

Congratulations are in order for **Tony March**, first place winner in Projects at the Science Fair which was held at Daytona Beach Junior College recently.

**Tony** also placed second when he gave an oral talk lasting twenty minutes on his project. Tony competed against 33 high school students.

**Tony** is a Senior and has been at Mainland for the last three years. He is very active in sports and is a member of the Varsity Football team, captain of the Wrestling team and a diver for the Swim team. **Tony** was also a member of the Buccaneer band for two years.

This is **Tony's** fourth year of Science fair competition. Tony earned money from previous fairs to build his winning project, and he also won an excellent award and two honorable mentions from his previous projects.

Unlike most of us who spend our summer leisurely ____ ____ Tony spent his summer wor____

*March 27, 1969*

his project which was **"The Semi-Micro Determinator of Carbon And Hydrogen In Organic Materials"**. The purpose of the project was to determine carbon and hydrogen in organic material. Many of the students in **Tony's** class thought that they would soon be getting a visit from the Florida State Beverage Commission because they thought that he was making still, and **Tony** explained this by stating that his project does not actually make alcohol but it determines the elements in it.

**Tony** feels that the teacher who has influenced him most in the field of science has been **Mrs. Mary Francis Aumiller**, who has taught him Chemistry for two years. When Tony was in Chemistry I, **Mrs. Aumiller** was the first

Accepting Grade 12
Science Fair Award

Brothers Gary, Tony, Bernard, and Gus—The 80s!

Sister, Mary

Aunt Katie—Matriarch
of the Family

Special invitee, Aunt Katie
helps Tony celebrate "Black Enterprise
Dealer of the Year" Award—1999

With Gail, the love of my life...

Attending one of many
General Motors dealer meetings.

Grand Opening of new Tony March
Buick/GMC/Saturn — Florida 1993

Touring Prince Rainier's private
automobile collection — Monaco 1988

Let's put a patent on this one!
In the backyard in Michigan.

Taking Crystal home from the hospital.
One proud papa.

Dad and daughter time. One of my favorite memories.

Tony and Crystal — All grown up.
Two peas in a pod.

Big Day! Celebrating Crystal's graduation
from the Mayo Medical School.

Tony as GM engineer — With associates, Bert Wanlass
and Mark Valenti, talking patents.

Tony, demonstrating one of his patent designs
to Pete Estes, President of General Motors.

Tony and GM President, Lloyd Ruess, signing agreement
to increase minority dealers by 40% — 1991

# 'Parade of Stars' raises $11 million for higher education

The United Negro College Fund launched its 50th anniversary last week, and raised $11 million in cash and pledges through the "Lou Rawls Parade of S Thousands residents t entertainr ganza that than 80 n the countr $135,000 v Connecticu

Throu ing effor "Parade of cast loca TV30, CPT radio sin United N Fund help ented youn ize their d lege educa lege Fund l costs of hi for most of dents atte

41 historically black colleges and universities.

"We are delighted that so many Americans called in during the show and pledged to help the

The show was also made possible by its national and founding sponsor Anheuser-Busch Companies. Additional support was provided by the Kellogg Company, American Airlines, AT&T, Avon, Church's Chicken, General

Motors Corporations. Special assistance was also given by American Urban Radio Networks, Walt Disney World, Westwood One Companies, Satellite Music Network and the Eight-Sheet Outdoor Advertising Association.

Tony (State Chairman for United Negro College Fund Telethon — Connecticut) presents check to Lou Rawls.

Tony March  sponsor

Tony "live" in studio — Hartford, Connecticut.
(National Lou Rawls Telethon for United Negro College Fund)

Original Pierce Buick dealership purchased in 1985. (It turned out not to be a dead end.)

Changing sign from Pierce Buick to Tony March Buick — 1985

The new Tony March Buick/GMC/Saturn — 1993

This is better than owning dealerships! With granddaughter, Amayah.

# Tony March
# 1996 Quality Dealer
# Award Winner

**Tony March**
**President**

**Tony March Buick-**
**GMC Truck-**
**Saturn**

**Hartford,**
**Connecticut**

For the past 26 years, TIME® Magazine and the National Automobile Dealers Association—in conjunction with The Goodyear Tire & Rubber Company for the past three years—have honored a select group of automobile dealers as recipients of the TIME Magazine Quality Dealer Award. TIME and Goodyear are pleased to name Tony March of Hartford, Connecticut a TIME Magazine Quality Dealer finalist for 1996, chosen for his exceptional performance as an automobile dealer and for his distinguished community service.

A native of Florida, Mr. March began his automotive career in 1971 in engineering with General Motors Fisher Body Division in Detroit, Michigan. In 1980, he became engineering group manager and shortly thereafter left General Motors to attend the GM Dealer Academy. Afterwards, Mr. March purchased Pierce Buick, Inc. in Hartford, Connecticut and renamed it Tony March Buick, Inc. Today, in addition to Buick, he also markets GMC Truck and the Saturn automotive lines.

Mr. March is active in his community, where he is director of the Greater Hartford YMCA and the state campaign chairman for the United Negro College Fund. He is also corporator of the Hartford Seminary, director of the Connecticut Sports Museum and serves on the Board of Regents for the University of Hartford. In addition, Mr. March has received many citizenship awards, including the Meritorious Service Award from the United Negro College Fund in recognition for this extensive fundraising efforts. He has also received the Business Leader of the Year Award from the Hartford Courant in recognition for business excellence and community interaction.

Mr. March has been a member of the Connecticut Automotive Trades Association since 1985 and currently serves as director. He is also director of his local automotive association, chairman of the GM Minority Dealer Council and a member of the GM Dealer Policy Council. Mr. March has received numerous automotive awards throughout his professional career, including the "Buick Best In Class" award.

TIME and Goodyear are proud to give this outstanding individual the recognition he has truly earned.

*TIME* magazine Quality Dealer Award recognition for exceptional dealership performance and distinguished community service.

Tony and Ernest Hodge
Cover photo for *Dealer Magazine* — 2005

"Perfect Attendance" car giveaway winner!

Groovin' with "Perfect Attendance" students.

Speaking with Hartford inner city housing resident
upon completion of $1 billion downtown redevelopment initiative.

Weaber High School has its own public adolescent health clinic!
Tony and Gail attending dedication.

Overseeing construction of downtown Hartford Science Center.

Reviewing new Science Center Exhibition concepts for
Hartford waterfront redevelopment initiative.

A newfound career. Tony in 2017 at Metropolitan Ministries, Tampa Bay, Florida.

A regular day
at the office...

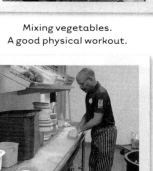

Mixing vegetables.
A good physical workout.

Tony cooking turkeys
for Thanksgiving, 2018.
6,000 meals served!

The never-ending
job of washing dishes
at the shelter.

A monster mash!
Cooking mashed potatoes.

CEO Tim Marks of Metropolitan
Ministries (far left) and board members
celebrate Tony graduating from
culinary school — 2017

First win!
(All of Tony's poker winnings are
donated to charitable causes.)

A passion for making a difference in the lives of young people. Encouraging
students to "dream in detail" and give back to help others.

At home among the homeless — St. Elizabeth Shelter, Hartford, Connecticut.
(It was outside of this building that friend and mentor
Paul Laffin was stabbed and died.)

Speaking with David, who was
once "one of them," on the streets
of Melbourne, Australia.

Preparing sandwiches
at Melbourne, Australia,
homeless shelter.

An early morning visit to a homeless
"tent city" — Oakland, California.